iCONLOGiC™

v061020
p204
9781944607609 (Perfect Bound Book)
9781944607616 (Coil Bound Book and PDF)
9781944607623 (eBook)

Articulate Storyline 360: The Essentials (2nd Edition)

"Skills and Drills" Learning

Kevin Siegel
Kal Hadi

Official

IconLogic Certified Articulate Storyline Developer

courseware

Get certified from the people who **literally** wrote the book on Articulate Storyline

https://www.iconlogic.com/instructor-led-training/certifications.html

iCONLOGiC

"Skills and Drills" Learning

Errata

Errata Detail

First version of this book (as indicated on the inside cover): v040120 published in April 2020

Second version of this book: v061020 published in June 2020. The corrections made to this version were largely cosmetic, fixed typographic errors, or added points of clarification.

- page 49: added a bullet to the first item in step 2 (the format was incorrect)
- page 54, step 2, changed the text from "Reuse content from the Notes window on a slide" to "Copy and paste content from MS Word onto a Storyline slide."
- page 68, step 2, added the word "is" before the word "selected."
- page 68, removed a misleading sentence from step 2
- page 68, updated the last paragraph to say "In summary, this trigger will take the learner to the next slide in the scene when the learner clicks the Start Button. Are you curious about the Conditions area? You'll explore this feature later."
- page 81, moved the image inline
- page 84, multiple typographic errors fixed
- page 85, added "to the States area" to the end of a sentence in the middle of the page
- page 88, changed the second sentence in the Confidence Check from "This time, when you hover above the image of the grain you'll see both a glow effect and the caption text." to "Hover your mouse above the image of the grain to see both the glow effect and the caption text."
- page 88, step 9, added a period at the end of the sentence
- page 89, fixed a few minor typographic errors
- page 100, added a new step 5 with instructions for formatting the text box
- page 100, new screen shot for step 6
- page 100, added a screenshot below step 9 showing a name typed into the Text Entry Field
- page 101, replaced the screenshot with an image that was cleaner
- page 103, moved the instruction to save (step 4) lower down (to step 7)
- page 104, made a word bold
- page 117, minor typographic error fixed
- page 122, added "for the Calculate button" to steps 3 and 4 to ensure clarity
- page 149, step 5, removed the words "slide 3.3"
- page 156, updated the name of the activity to "Insert a Matching Drop-down Slide"

iCONLOGiC
"Skills and Drills" Learning

Contents

NOTES

NOTES

iCONLOGiC

"Skills and Drills" Learning

About This Book

This Section Contains Information About:

- The Authors, page viii
- IconLogic, page viii
- Book Conventions, page ix
- Confidence Checks, page ix
- Book and Storyline System Requirements, page ix
- Storyline Projects and Assets (Data Files), page x
- How Articulate 360 Updates Affect This Book, page xi
- Contacting IconLogic, page xi

NOTES

The Authors

Kevin Siegel is a Certified Master Trainer (CMT), Certified Technical Trainer (CTT+), and Certified Online Training Professional (COTP). Following a successful tour of duty with the U.S. Coast Guard (where Kevin was twice decorated with the Coast Guard's Achievement Medal), he has spent decades as a technical communicator, classroom and online trainer, eLearning developer, publisher, and public speaker. Kevin, who founded IconLogic, Inc., in the early 1990s, has written hundreds of training books for adult learners.

Some of his best-selling books include "Adobe Captivate: The Essentials," "Articulate Storyline: The Essentials," and "TechSmith Camtasia: The Essentials." Kevin has also been recognized by Adobe as one of the top trainers worldwide.

Kal Hadi is a Certified Technical Trainer (CTT+) and Certified Online Training Professional (COTP) with more than 20 years of experience in computer graphics, imaging, and electronic publishing. Kal is a graduate of the Rochester Institute of Technology Electronic Publishing graduate program. He is also the author of many books and papers in graphics and web publishing, including multiple books on Articulate Storyline.

IconLogic

Founded in 1992, IconLogic is a training, development, and publishing company offering services to clients across the globe.

As a **training** company, IconLogic has directly trained tens of thousands of professionals both on-site and online on dozens of applications. Our training clients include some of the largest companies in the world including Adobe Systems, Inc., Urogen, Agilent, Sanofi Pasteur, Kelsey Seybold, FAA, Office Pro, Adventist Health Systems, AGA, AAA, Wells Fargo, VA.gov, American Express, Lockheed Martin, General Mills, Grange Insurance, Electric Boat, Michigan.gov, Freddie Mac, Fannie Mae, ADP, ADT, Federal Reserve Bank of Richmond, Walmart, Kroger, Duke Energy, USCG, USMC, Canadian Blood, PSA, Department of Homeland Security, and the Department of Defense.

As a **development** company, IconLogic has produced eLearning and technical documentation for Duke Energy, World Bank, Heineken, EverFi, Bank of America, Fresenius Kabi, Wells Fargo, Federal Express, Fannie Mae, American Express, Microsoft, Department of For-Hire Vehicles, DC Child and Family Services, DCORM, Canadian Blood, Cancer.org, MLB, Archrock, NEEF, CHUBB, Canadian Natural Resources, and Hagerty Insurance.

As a **publishing** company, IconLogic has published hundreds of critically acclaimed books and created technical documents for both print and digital publication. Some of our most popular titles over the years include books on HTML, Dreamweaver, QuarkXPress, PageMaker, InDesign, Word, Excel, Access, Publisher, RoboHelp, RoboDemo, iSpring, Presenter, Storyline, Captivate, and PowerPoint for eLearning.

You can learn more about IconLogic's varied services at www.iconlogic.com.

Book Conventions

In our experience, humans learn best by doing, not just by watching or listening. With this concept in mind, instructors and authors with years of experience training adult learners have created IconLogic books. IconLogic books typically contain a minimal amount of text and are loaded with hands-on activities, screen captures, and challenge exercises to reinforce newly acquired skills. This book is divided into modules. Because each module builds on lessons learned in a previous module, it is recommended that you complete each module in succession.

Lesson Key

Instructions for you to follow look like this:

❑ choose **File > Open**

If you are expected to type anything or if something is important, it is set in bold type like this:

❑ type **9** into the text field

If you are expected to press a key on your keyboard, the instruction looks like this:

❑ press [**shift**]

Confidence Checks

As you work through this book, you will come across the image at the right (which indicates a Confidence Check). Throughout each module, you are guided through hands-on, step-by-step activities. To help ensure that you are understanding the book's content, Confidence Checks encourage you to complete a process or steps on your own (without step-by-step guidance). Because some of the book's activities build on completed Confidence Checks, you should complete each of the Confidence Checks in order.

Book and Storyline System Requirements

This book teaches you how to use Articulate Storyline 360, which is part of the Articulate 360 suite of applications. You can download a free 30-day trial of Storyline or purchase the subscription at **https://articulate.com/360**.

Once you have installed Articulate 360, you will have access to Articulate Storyline 360. According to Articulate, the following are the system requirements to use Storyline 360.

Hardware: CPU, 2.0 GHz processor or higher (32-bit or 64-bit). Memory, 2 GB minimum. Available Disk Space, 1 GB minimum. Display, 1,280 x 800 screen resolution or higher. Multimedia, Sound card, microphone, and webcam to record video and/or narration.

Software: Windows 7 (32-bit or 64-bit), Windows 8 (32-bit or 64-bit), or Windows 10 (32-bit or 64-bit).

Backward Compatibility: Storyline 1 and Storyline 2 projects can be upgraded to Storyline 360. Storyline 360 projects cannot be opened or edited with older Storyline versions.

Importing Content: Microsoft PowerPoint 2010 or later (32-bit or 64-bit), Articulate Presenter '09, '13, or 360, Articulate Quizmaker '09, '13, or 360, Articulate Engage '09, '13, or 360.

Publishing to Word: Microsoft Word 2010 or later (32-bit or 64-bit).

Translation: Microsoft Word 2010 or later (32-bit or 64-bit).

NOTES

Storyline Projects and Assets (Data Files)

This book assumes that you have never used Articulate Storyline 360 before and that you don't have anything to create Storyline eLearning besides Storyline 360 and a willingness to learn. This book teaches you how to use Storyline 360, step by step. The book also includes free project files and supporting assets, such as images, videos, and audio files that comprise typical eLearning courses.

Ready to get started? Let's begin by downloading the assets (data files) from the IconLogic server that you'll need for the projects in the book.

Download Data Files

1. Download the student data files necessary to complete the lessons presented in this book.

   ☐ start a web browser and visit the following web address: **http://www.iconlogic.com/pc**

   ☐ scroll down to the **Articulate Storyline Data Files** section

   ☐ click the **Articulate Storyline 360: The Essentials (2nd Edition)** link

   The download is a zipped file containing several folders and files. On most web browsers, a dialog box opens asking if you want to Save or Open the file. The image below is the dialog box you'll see if you use Firefox. We suggest that you Save the file to your computer (the desktop is ideal).

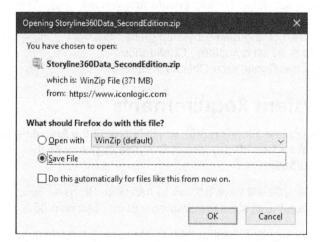

2. Save the ZIP file to your computer.

3. Once the file fully downloads, close the web browser.

4. Locate the **Storyline360Data_SecondEdition** ZIP file you just downloaded to your computer and unzip the file (we suggest extracting the files to your desktop).

   The unzipped data files should now be on your computer within a folder named **Storyline360Data_SecondEdition**. As you move through the lessons in this book, you will be working with these files.

How Articulate 360 Updates Affect This Book

Articulate releases updates to the Articulate 360 suite of applications which may cause a mismatch between what is shown in this book and on screen.

If something on your screen does not match what we show in this book, visit our Articulate Storyline page on the IconLogic website for possible book updates or errata information at: www.iconlogic.com/articulate-storyline-360-essentials-second-edition-workbook.html.

Should you get stuck and find no relief on your own or from the IconLogic website (www.iconlogic.com/articulate-storyline-360-essentials-second-edition-workbook.html), email Kevin or Kal directly for clarification. You can reach Kevin at **ksiegel@iconlogic.com** and Kal at **kal@amananet.com**.

Special Thanks

We truly appreciate the work of the proofreaders and beta testers who labored diligently to find as many typos and errors as possible in both this book and the supporting project files. Specifically, we would like to thank **Ellie Abrams**, **Martin Rosoff**, **Amanda Christianson**, **Janay White**, **Victoria Hokana**, **Dan Earley**, **Patty DeLuca**, and **Don Finch** for their efforts.

Contacting IconLogic

Web: www.iconlogic.com
Email Kevin: ksiegel@iconlogic.com
Email Kal: kal@amananet.com
Phone: 410.956.4949, ext 711

NOTES

Notes

iCONLOGiC

"Skills and Drills" Learning

Rank Your Skills

Before starting this book, complete the skills assessment on the next page.

Skills Assessment

How This Assessment Works

Ten course objectives for *Articulate Storyline 360: The Essentials* (2nd edition) are listed below. **Before starting the book**, review each objective and rank your skills using the scale next to each objective. A rank of ① means **No Confidence** in the skill. A rank of ⑤ means **Total Confidence**. After you've completed this assessment, work through the entire book. **After finishing the book**, review each objective and rank your skills now that you've completed the book. Most people see dramatic improvements in the second assessment after completing the lessons in this book.

Before-Class Skills Assessment

	No Confidence			Confidence	
1. I can redock Storyline's windows.	①	②	③	④	⑤
2. I can add a Trigger to a slide object.	①	②	③	④	⑤
3. I can edit a Slide Master.	①	②	③	④	⑤
4. I can insert a Character.	①	②	③	④	⑤
5. I can create a Conditional Trigger.	①	②	③	④	⑤
6. I can create a Variable.	①	②	③	④	⑤
7. I can create a Quiz.	①	②	③	④	⑤
8. I can add a Motion Path.	①	②	③	④	⑤
9. I can create a Drag-and-Drop question.	①	②	③	④	⑤
10. I can Publish as HTML5.	①	②	③	④	⑤

After-Class Skills Assessment

	No Confidence			Confidence	
1. I can redock Storyline's windows.	①	②	③	④	⑤
2. I can add a Trigger to a slide object.	①	②	③	④	⑤
3. I can edit a Slide Master.	①	②	③	④	⑤
4. I can insert a Character.	①	②	③	④	⑤
5. I can create a Conditional Trigger.	①	②	③	④	⑤
6. I can create a Variable.	①	②	③	④	⑤
7. I can create a Quiz.	①	②	③	④	⑤
8. I can add a Motion Path.	①	②	③	④	⑤
9. I can create a Drag-and-Drop question.	①	②	③	④	⑤
10. I can Publish as HTML5.	①	②	③	④	⑤

iCONLOGiC

"Skills and Drills" Learning

Preface

In This Module You Will Learn About:

About Articulate 360 and Storyline 360

Articulate 360 is a suite of tools developed by Articulate (www.articulate.com). The tools include **Storyline 360** (which is the focus of this book), **Studio 360** (a collection of eLearning products, including **Presenter**, **Engage**, and **Quiz Maker**), **Replay 360** (a screen recording tool useful for making video demos), and **Peek** (a desktop application that lets you record either Mac or PC screens). There are web-based applications as well, including **Rise** (a template-based online authoring tool for creating very simple and responsive courses), and **Review** (an online-based course review process where team members can comment and provide feedback).

When you start Articulate 360, you see the following application Launcher screen:

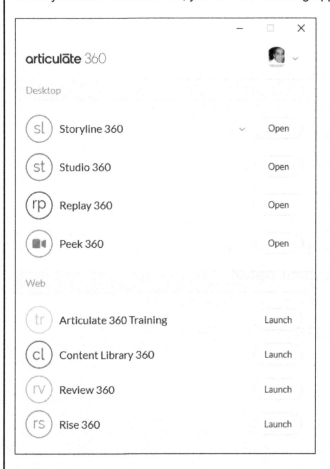

To use any of the tools that comprise Articulate 360, you must subscribe to the suite via Articulate's website (www.articulate.com). To edit existing projects, or create new content, you need to keep your Articulate 360 subscription active.

In addition to the tools mentioned above, Articulate 360 includes the Content Library 360 containing a vast selection of professional templates, images, and other digital learning assets.

Planning eLearning Projects

If you want to create eLearning, Storyline is an essential development tool. However, if your goal is effective and relevant eLearning, you'll need more than Storyline. Consider the following:

☐ **Why are you creating an eLearning course?** You'd be surprised how many people start Storyline and just start creating content. This kind of development process might be well intentioned, but you really need to map out the entire course, including the way you are going to track learner comprehension (if that's important to you). During the mapping process, you might conclude that your course isn't appropriate for eLearning and move on to another course.

☐ **Who is your audience?** The way you teach children is different from the way you teach adults. For instance, children need praise and encouragement during the learning process; however, adult learners might find such praise and encouragement annoying.

☐ **What exactly are you teaching, and is it appropriate for eLearning?** Not every lesson in an instructor-led course can be effectively re-tooled for eLearning. For instance, if a course relies on breakout groups, group discussion, or collaborative work, those aspects of the course cannot easily be included in eLearning. Keep in mind that eLearners almost always work on their own with little or no interaction with a colleague.

☐ **Does your project need to accommodate learners with special needs?** If the answer is yes, you should budget approximately 30 percent more time to produce accessible eLearning.

☐ **Do you want your projects to contain images, videos, and background music?** If so, where will you get them? Also, are you going to use a template? If so, who is going to design and create it?

☐ **Will there be annotations (written instructions and descriptions)?** If so, who will write the content for the annotations? Do you need an eLearning script? Do you need a voiceover script?

☐ **Is your course soft skills, or is it a software simulation?** If it is soft skills, does it make sense to create most of the content in Microsoft PowerPoint and then import the presentation into Storyline?

Budgeting eLearning Projects

Many new Storyline developers underestimate the time needed to produce projects. Although it is certainly easier and faster to create eLearning content than ever before, it still takes time. To determine your level of effort, the first thing you need to know is the total play time in minutes of your eLearning course. Once you have that number, you can calculate your level of effort.

As an example, let's calculate how long it's going to take you to produce a 60-minute eLearning course. Because you don't want to create a single project that, when published, plays for 60 consecutive minutes, it's ideal to break the 60 minutes of content into chunks. We suggest that each chunk play for no more than five minutes. That means you will have 12, five-minute lessons (or modules).

If you need to write the content for the course (somebody has to), you'll need a script (page 11) and/or storyboard (page 12); and, if there's voiceover audio, you'll need a voiceover script. It could easily take you three hours to write a script to support each five-minute eLearning lesson. Therefore, you should budget at least 36 hours to write the entire one-hour eLearning course (12 x 3=36). Depending on how fast you write, you could easily double those hours, meaning you may need to budget 80 hours for the writing.

In our experience, writing a voiceover script is easier than writing a step-by-step main script (voiceover scripts typically take us 50 percent less time to write). If you spent 80 hours writing the script, you should budget 40 hours to write the voiceover script. Once the voiceover script is done, you'll also need to include time for recording the voice-overs, making corrections to the script post-rehearsal, and recording the simulations using Storyline.

Next comes the production process where you will need to add slide text (annotations) and images, interactivity, triggers, hotspots, variables, audio, animations, videos, software simulations or demonstrations, quizzes, and more. You should budget approximately two hours of labor to produce every single minute of eLearning in Storyline. Therefore, it could easily take 10 hours to produce a five-minute module.

During the production process (detailed beginning on page 5), you'll likely add audio or record audio files. And you may need to edit the audio files by performing common tasks such as removing unwanted noise.

When you are done producing the project, you will publish the finished lesson, upload the published assets to a server or Learning Management System, and test for scoring or interactivity errors. If errors are found, you'll need to return to Storyline to fix problems. After fixing those problems, you'll need to republish, repost, and then retest.

An eLearning development budget for a 60-minute eLearning course might look something like this:

- ☐ 40-80 hours to write an eLearning script or create the storyboard to support 12, five-minute lessons for a one-hour course

- ☐ 120 hours to edit, produce, and test 12, five-minute lessons

- ☐ 20-40 hours to write a voiceover script to be used by your narrator

- ☐ 20-40 hours to record and enhance your own voiceover audio

eLearning Development Phases

The infographic below offers a visual way to think about the eLearning development process and phases. A larger version of the graphic can be downloaded from www.iconlogic.com/skills-drills-workbooks/elearning-resources.html.

eLearning Development Phases

1 DISCOVERY

Meet with the client. Find out **what they want** in an ideal eLearning course. Who is the **audience**? Define a course **mission statement** for the course in general. You'll also need a mission statement for each lesson in the course. Will the course require **accessibility**? **Audio**? Will it need to be **localized**? What kind of **hardware** will students be using to access the course?

2 DESIGN

Which tool will you be using to develop the content (**Captivate**, **PowerPoint**, **Presenter**, **Storyline**, or perhaps a combination of a couple tools)? **Instructional design**, a **graphical treatment**, and **navigational choices** are now made and implemented.

3 WRITING and/or STORYBOARDING

Now that you have chosen a production tool and decided the overall design of the course, you'll need to **plot out the flow** of the course and **write a script and/or a storyboard**. If the course includes voiceover audio, you'll need a separate (and different) script for that.

4 PRODUCTION

Now it's time to get busy with the **development work** in the selected tool. This includes everything right up to the point of publishing. You'll also **beta test** the lessons in this phase as they are completed.

5 CLIENT APPROVAL

You're almost there! But, before project completion, you'll need to get your **client's approval**. Depending upon how this goes, **you may need to repeat** parts of **steps two, three, and four**.

6 PUBLISHING and IMPLEMENTATION

This includes not only **publishing locally**, but uploading the content to a **web server** or **LMS (SCORM or AICC)**. Be sure to allow time to work out bugs in this phase.

7 MAINTENANCE

You did a great job! But sometimes changes and updates are necessary. This phase includes **making updates** to the content and **re-posting to the LMS or web server**.

Brought to you by:

iCONLOGiC
www.iconlogic.com

NOTES

NOTES

eLearning Development Process

We've listed the typical eLearning development process below. The list includes a skill level number indicating the level of difficulty for each task. The numbers range from 1 to 10, with 10 indicating the most difficult task.

☐ **Write It:** Depending on the type of eLearning you're creating, you may need multiple scripts. If you're creating a **soft skills** lesson (life lessons such as conflict resolution or on-boarding), you'll likely need a storyboard (see page 12) and a voiceover script. If you're creating software simulations (something we cover in-depth during our "Articulate Storyline 360: Beyond the Essentials, Third Edition" book), you need the detailed instructions necessary to record the simulation with Storyline (see page 11). *The writing phase is the most important step in the process.* Without good scripts, you don't have a good movie. Think we're kidding? The lack of a viable script doomed movie classics such as *Battlefield Earth*, *Barb Wire*, *Heaven's Gate*, *Popeye,* and *Ishtar*. *(Skill Level: 10)*

☐ **Rehearse It:** If you're creating a software simulation, go through the script with the software you'll be recording in front of you. Don't skip any steps. You'll be able to see if the steps in the script are incomplete or inaccurate before you attempt to record the steps using Storyline. *(Skill Level: 2)*

☐ **Reset It:** After rehearsing a software simulation, be sure to "undo" everything you did during the rehearsal. When you ultimately use Storyline to record the actual software simulation few things are more frustrating than coming across steps that have already been completed (requiring you to stop the recording and re-record). *(Skill Level: 1)*

☐ **Record It:** If rehearsals go well, recording the software simulation should be easy. *(Skill Level: 2)*

☐ **Produce It:** In this task you add captions, highlight boxes, text entry fields, spell check, add buttons, click boxes, animations, quizzes, audio, variables, triggers, conditional triggers, etc. *(Skill Level: 8)*

☐ **Publish It:** Although not a difficult task, if your project is large (lots of slides and audio), publishing could take some time. You cannot do any work in Storyline while your project is publishing. *(Skill Level: 1)*

☐ **Post It:** This is a broad category. Posting your project means different things depending on where your finished lessons are supposed to go. For instance, if your lessons are supposed to be uploaded into a Learning Management System (LMS), you have to set up the reporting features in Storyline, publish the project, and then upload it into the LMS. Then you need to test the lesson to ensure it scores correctly. If you plan to simply add the lessons to a web server, posting may be as easy as handing the published files off to your webmaster. *(Skill Level: 2 or 3... or higher if your LMS is difficult to use)*

☐ **Test It:** This task isn't difficult, but it could take time. If you find a problem, you've got to go back and fix it, publish it, and then retest it. Some people argue that this step belongs above the **Publish It** process. We cannot argue with that logic. However, after testing the project, you still need to publish it, and as we mentioned above, if you're working with an LMS, upload it and test again. *(Skill Level: 2)*

☐ **Republish, Repost, Retest:** If something doesn't work when you test the posted version of your lesson, you have to return to Storyline and fix the problem. After that, you'll Publish, Post, and Test again. *(Skill Level: 2 or 3... or higher if you can't resolve the problem)*

Designing Storyline Slides

Because much of the Storyline interface is similar to Microsoft PowerPoint, if you have used PowerPoint, Storyline may seem familiar to you. When working in PowerPoint, you insert slides when you need them and then populate those slides with text, images, animations... just about anything. The same is true when working in Storyline.

Of course, there are big differences between PowerPoint and Storyline, and you'll discover those differences as you work through this book. What the two programs have in common is your ability to apply themes that quickly create visually-appealing slides with a click of your mouse. While those themes help make the slides look good, they also need to effectively convey your message. When it comes to building effective slides, here are a few things to think about:

- ☐ **Bulleted Lists.** There are certain occasions when a bulleted list is the best way to convey an idea. However, just because PowerPoint uses a bulleted approach to information by default doesn't mean you have to use that format in Storyline.

- ☐ **Break Things Up.** Try splitting the bullets up into separate slides with a single image to illustrate each point, or forgo the text altogether and replace it with a chart, diagram, or other informative image.

- ☐ **Less is More.** It is not necessary to have every bit of information you discuss also appear on the slide. Encourage your audience to listen and, if necessary, take notes based on what you say, not what is displayed on the slide.

- ☐ **To Animation or Not to Animate.** Like PowerPoint, you can add animations to just about anything and everything on a Storyline slide. However, we suggest keeping animations to a minimum. While animations can be cool, they can distracting. And nothing says "High School Presentation Circa 1997" quite like a dancing animated image clumsily plopped on a rainbow gradient background.

- ☐ **Simplify.** eLearning lessons are plentiful—particularly bad ones. Trust us, your learner will not be impressed with how many moving, colorful parts each slide contains.

- ☐ **Photos vs. Images.** Consider taking more of a photographic approach to the images you use. You can easily find stock photographs on the web using any one of a number of pay-for-use websites. There are many free sites, but keep in mind that to save time and frustration (and improve on the selection and quality), you might want to set aside a budget to pay for images.

Fonts and Learning

There is no denying that the most important thing about eLearning is solid content. Read on to discover the many surprising ways fonts can affect your content.

Some Fonts Read Better On-Screen

eCommerce Consultant Dr. Ralph F. Wilson did a study in 2001 to determine if serif fonts (fonts with little lines on the tops and bottoms of characters, such as Times New Roman) or sans serif fonts (those without lines, such as Arial) were more suited to being read on computer monitors. His study concluded that although Times New Roman is easily read in printed materials, the lower resolution of monitors (72 dots per inch (dpi) versus 180 dpi or higher) makes it much more difficult to read in digital format. Arial 12 pt was compared to Times New Roman 12 pt with respondents finding the sans serif Arial font more readable at a rate of two to one.

Lorem ipsum frangali puttuto rigali fortuitous confulence magficati alorem. Lorem ipsum frangali puttuto rigali fortuitous confulence magficati alorem.	Lorem ipsum frangali puttuto rigali fortuitous confulence magficati alorem. Lorem ipsum frangali puttuto rigali fortuitous confulence magficati alorem.
Times New Roman 12 pt	Arial 12 pt

Source: https://www.practicalecommerce.com/html-email-fonts

Wilson also tested the readability of Arial versus Verdana on computer screens and found that in font sizes greater than 10 pt, Arial was more readable, whereas Verdana was more readable in font sizes 10 pt and smaller.

So should you stop using Times New Roman in your eLearning lessons? Not completely. For instance, you can still use Times New Roman for text content that is not expected to be skimmed over quickly or read in a hurry.

The Readability of Fonts Affects Participation

A study done at the University of Michigan in 2008 on typecase in instructions found that the ease with which a font in instructional material is read can have an impact on the perceived skill level needed to complete a task.

The study found that if directions are presented in a font that is deemed more difficult to read, "the task will be viewed as being difficult, taking a long time to complete and perhaps, not even worth trying."

The results of the study by Wilson indicate that it is probably not a good idea to present eLearning material, especially to beginners, in a Times New Roman font, as it may make the information seem too difficult to process or overwhelming.

Most Popular Fonts

We polled our "Logical" newsletter readers and asked which fonts they tended to use in eLearning. Here is a list of the most popular fonts:

- ❏ Verdana
- ❏ Helvetica
- ❏ Arial
- ❏ Calibri
- ❏ Times
- ❏ Palatino
- ❏ Times New Roman
- ❏ Century Schoolbook (for print)

Fonts and Personas

If you are creating eLearning for business professionals, you might want to use a different font in your design than you would if you were creating eLearning for high school students. But what font would you use if you wanted to convey a feeling of happiness? Formality?

In a study funded by Microsoft by A. Dawn Shaikh, Barbara S. Chaparro, and Doug Fox, the perceived personality traits of fonts were categorized. The table below shows the top three fonts for each personality objective.

	Top Three		
Stable	TNR	Arial	Cambria
Flexible	Kristen	Gigi	Rage Italic
Conformist	Courier New	TNR	Arial
Polite	Monotype Corsiva	TNR	Cambria
Mature	TNR	Courier New	Cambria
Formal	TNR	Monotype Corsiva	Georgia
Assertive	**Impact**	**Rockwell Xbold**	Georgia
Practical	Georgia	TNR	Cambria
Creative	Gigi	Kristen	Rage Italic
Happy	Kristen	Gigi	Comic Sans
Exciting	Gigi	Kristen	Rage Italic
Attractive	Monotype Corsiva	Rage Italic	Gigi
Elegant	Monotype Corsiva	Rage Italic	Gigi
Cuddly	Kristen	Gigi	Comic Sans
Feminine	Gigi	Monotype Corsiva	Kristen
Unstable	Gigi	Kristen	Rage Italic
Rigid	**Impact**	Courier New	Agency FB
Rebel	Gigi	Kristen	Rage Italic
Rude	**Impact**	**Rockwell Xbold**	Agency FB
Youthful	Kristen	Gigi	Comic Sans
Casual	Kristen	Comic Sans	Gigi
Passive	Kristen	Gigi	Comic Sans
Impractical	Gigi	Rage Italic	Kristen
Unimaginative	Courier New	Arial	Consolas
Sad	**Impact**	Courier New	Agency FB
Dull	Courier New	Consolas	Verdana
Unattractive	**Impact**	Courier New	**Rockwell Xbold**
Plain	Courier New	**Impact**	**Rockwell Xbold**
Coarse	**Impact**	**Rockwell Xbold**	Courier New
Masculine	**Impact**	**Rockwell Xbold**	Courier New

Source: https://soma.sbcc.edu/users/Russotti/113/personality_Shaikh.pdf

Scripts for Software Simulations

When we have created text-based eLearning scripts or received them from clients, we've generally seen them in two flavors: paragraphs and tables.

Scripts in Paragraph Format

If you are creating a script for eLearning, your text should be formatted in a way that is easy to follow. You can format the script in paragraphs, but you will need to clearly label the parts. You may find that formatted paragraphs are all you need. However, we recommend a table or grid format for a script that will be developed into eLearning.

Step 1

Screen: Display the document

Action: Move the cursor to the Format menu and click Format

Caption: Click Format

Voiceover: Now let's open the Format menu to get started with formatting the document.

Scripts in Table Format

Below is a picture of a script used to create an eLearning lesson. The script was created in Microsoft Word and is available in the Storyline360Data_SecondEdition folder (the file is called **SampleScript**).

iCONLOGiC
3320 Breckenridge Way
Riva, MD 21140
410.956.4949 | Fax: 443.782.2366

Sample Script for Recording Screen Actions with Storyline

Lesson Name: Print a NotePad File with Landscape Orientation

Step	Screen	Action to be Taken by Storyline Developer	Caption Text	Narrator Says
1)	A NotePad file should be open prior to recording. You can start NotePad by choose Start > Run and typing notepad. Any open NotePad document can be used for this simulation.	Pull a screen shot of the NotePad file do not click anything. This slide will contain some introductory narrative.	During this lesson you will learn how to print a NotePad document	During this lesson you will learn how to print a NotePad document in Landscape Orientation.
2)	A NotePad file is open. Nothing should be selected and no menus should be open.	Click the **File** menu	First, let's display the Print dialog box. Choose **File > Print**.	To begin, let's display the Print dialog box by choosing the Print command from the File menu.

NOTES

Storyboarding for Soft Skills

When the training objective is a soft skill, such as how to interact with others in the workplace or how to comply with legally required behavior, there may be no step-by-step process to spell out. Instead, you have to describe and demonstrate the behavior in a way that engages the learner. This is where the screen-writing part of writing training materials comes into play.

You can present soft skills through slides or videos. Either way, the writing must be both clear and engaging.

Here is a typical plotline for soft skills training.

❑ State a real-world problem, challenge, or requirement

❑ Illustrate what happens on failure

❑ Demonstrate and describe how to succeed

❑ Include a quiz or other evaluation

A storyboard, which can be made up of images, text, or both, allows you to plan what is pictured or acted out, as well as what is said for each slide or scene.

Even if you are not an artist, you can sketch the basics of the characters, setting, and behavior for each scene. Take a look at the image below. We think you will agree that the drawings are not works of art. Nevertheless, you can tell that they depict two people meeting in the reception area of an office. (You'll find a sample storyboard in the Storyline360Data_SecondEdition folder.)

Slide/ Scene No.	Picture	Voiceover	Action	Dialogue
1				
2				
3				

iCONLOGiC
"Skills and Drills" Learning

Module 1: Exploring Storyline

In This Module You Will Learn About:

- The Storyline Interface, page 14
- Previewing, page 22

And You Will Learn To:

- Explore a Finished Storyline Project, page 14
- Explore Slides and Windows, page 16
- Zoom and Magnify, page 18
- Explore Panels, page 20
- Preview the Entire Project, page 22

The Storyline Interface

As you work through the lessons in this book, the goal is to get you comfortable with each specific Storyline area or feature before proceeding. Like any feature-rich program, mastering Storyline is going to be a marathon, not a sprint. Soon enough, you'll be in full stride, creating awesome eLearning content using Storyline. But before the run comes the warm up. During these first few activities, you will familiarize yourself with Storyline's user interface. Specifically, you'll be instructed to start Storyline, open an existing project, and explore Storyline's interface a bit.

Guided Activity 1: Explore a Finished Storyline Project

1. Start Articulate 360 and then Storyline 360.

   The Articulate 360 Launcher opens providing access to all of the Articulate 360 Desktop and Web tools.

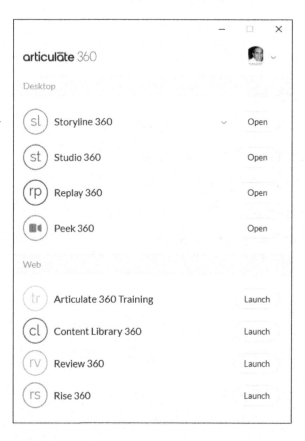

   ☐ on the **Launcher**, click **Open** to the right of **Storyline 360**

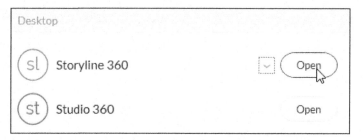

   Note: You can start Articulate Storyline 360 independent of the Launcher shown in the first image above. However, if you access the Launcher first you'll always be notified if there's an update available for any of the tools that make up the Articulate 360 suite.

Shown below is the initial screen you'll see after you start Storyline 360. At the top left are quick links to start a New Project, Record the Screen, and Import content from other sources. If you've opened existing Storyline projects, those projects will be available in the **Recent** area. Beneath the Recent projects, you'll find a **Browse for more** link that will let you find and open existing Storyline projects (you'll be using that link next).

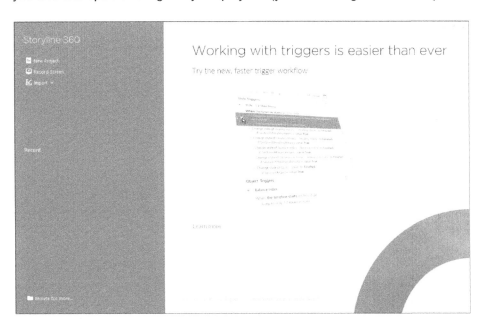

2. Open an existing Storyline 360 project from the **Storyline360Data_SecondEdition** folder.

   ☐ at the **bottom left** of the screen, click **Browse for more**

   The **Open** dialog box appears.

   ☐ navigate to the **Storyline360Data_SecondEdition** folder and open **Finished_Chesapeake_Stables_Project.story**

   The project opens. During the lessons presented in this book, you will learn how to create this eLearning course from scratch. It introduces you to a horse-boarding facility named Chesapeake Stables.

3. Close the project and reopen it using the Recent area.

   ☐ choose **File > Close** (do not save the project if prompted)

   ☐ from the **Recent** area, click **Finished_Chesapeake_Stables_Project**

By default, Storyline projects open in Story View.

Guided Activity 2: Explore Slides and Windows

1. Ensure that the **Finished_Chesapeake_Stables_Project** project is still open.

2. Explore slides and scenes.

   ☐ from the top of the Storyline window, double-click the slide labeled **1.1 A Guide to Our Facilities**

The Storyline window changes from Story View to Slide View. At the left you'll see slide thumbnails and a Scenes drop-down menu. The slide you double-clicked is open in the middle of the screen. At the right you'll see some panels with additional options.

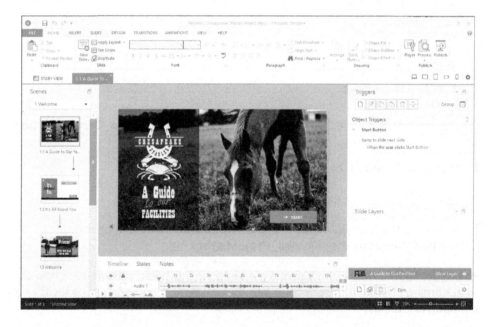

   ☐ from the left side of the Storyline window, click the **Scenes** drop-down menu and choose **2 Farm Culture**

This project consists of seven scenes (a scene is a collection of related slides). You'll learn more about the relationship between scenes and slides beginning in the next module when you create your first project from scratch and begin adding content.

Scenes Confidence Check

1. Still working in the **Finished_Chesapeake_Stables_Project** file, spend a few moments exploring each of the seven scenes.

2. As you move from scene to scene, click and explore each of the slides within those scenes.

3. When finished exploring, close any open slides to return to Story View. (Note that open slides can be closed via the Close box in the slide's title tab, which is shown below.)

When you're in Story View, you'll see the Story View tab at the left of the Storyline window.

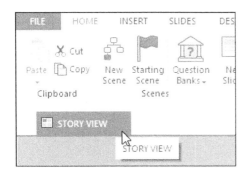

Guided Activity 3: Zoom and Magnify

1. Ensure that the **Finished_Chesapeake_Stables_Project** project is still open.

2. Open a slide.

   ☐ from the middle of the Story View window, double-click the slide labeled **3.1 Farm Services**

3. Zoom closer to the slide.

   ☐ click the **View** tab on the **Ribbon**

   ☐ from the **Zoom** group, click **Zoom**

   The Zoom dialog box opens.

   ☐ select **200%**

   Zoom to:
   - ◯ Fit
   - ◯ 400%
   - ◉ 200%

   ☐ click the **OK** button

   Being this close to the slide makes it easer to view and edit the slide's content. At this zoom percent, you will need to use the scroll bars to move around the slide.

4. Change the slide zoom by using the Zoom slider.

   ☐ at the lower right of the Storyline window, drag the zoom slider **left** to zoom out

Note: You can also click the plus and minus signs to change the Zoom.

5. Change the slide zoom to Fit in Window.

   ☐ from the **Zoom** group (on the **View** tab of the **Ribbon**), click **Fit to Window**

Note: You can zoom as far away from a slide as **10** percent and as close as **400** percent.

6. Close the slide to return to Story View.

Guided Activity 4: Explore Panels

1. Ensure that the **Finished_Chesapeake_Stables_Project** file is still open.

2. Open a slide.

   ☐ from the **Story View** window, scroll down and double-click the slide labeled **5.1 Feed Your Horse**

3. Undock the Timeline panel.

   ☐ from the bottom of the Storyline window, drag the word **Timeline** to the middle of the window

   The Timeline panel detaches from the bottom of the window and floats in its own window.

4. Undock the Triggers panel.

   ☐ from the right of the Storyline window, drag the word **Triggers** to the middle of the window

   Now both the Timeline and Trigger panel are detached and floating in their own windows. Using this technique, you can customize the look and feel of the Storyline window based on the size of your computer display.

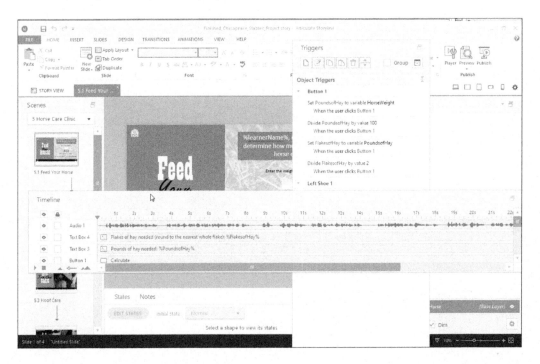

5. Redock all windows.

   ☐ select the **View** tab on the Ribbon

   ☐ from the **Grid and Guides** group, click **Redock All Windows**

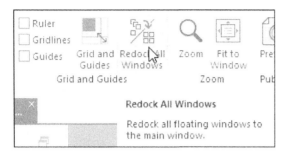

   All of the panels (windows) return to their default locations.

6. Resize the Timeline panel.

   ☐ from the bottom of the Storyline window, drag the **Timeline** to the middle of screen

   ☐ resize the Timeline as necessary to see all of its objects

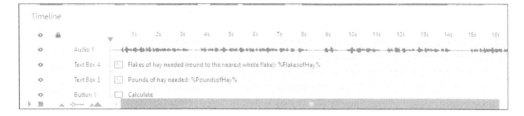

   The Timeline allows you to control when slide objects appear onscreen. You'll use with the Timeline throughout this book.

Panels Confidence Check

1. Still working in the **Finished_Chesapeake_Stables_Project** file, spend a few moments exploring some of the other panels/windows.

2. Undock some of the panels/windows (position them anywhere you want on your screen).

3. Redock all of the windows.

4. Close any open slides to return to Story View.

Previewing

During the activities presented in this book, you will learn how to create the Chesapeake Stables project from scratch. At some point, you will finish the development process by publishing the project. Once published, the output can be viewed by learners on all kinds of devices (including desktop computers, laptops, smart phones, and tablets.

Prior to publishing a project, it's a good idea to preview the project so you can see how the content will look once published. Storyline includes multiple Preview options including Slide, Scene, and Project.

Guided Activity 5: Preview the Entire Project

1. Ensure that the **Finished_Chesapeake_Stables_Project** project is still open.

2. Preview the project.

    ☐ select the **Home** tab on the Ribbon

    ☐ from the **Publish** area, click the bottom part of the **Preview** icon (the arrow)

    ☐ choose **Entire Project**

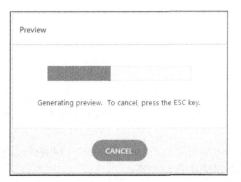

The project is generated and opens in a Preview window. Most of the slides are interactive to some degree (there are slides with interactive buttons; others contain videos or drag-and-drop interactions).

3. Preview the Responsive Playback options.

   ☐ ensure the Preview window is open

   By default, you are previewing the project as a desktop user. However, Storyline projects can be used by learners on several types of devices. You can use the Preview window to get an idea of how your content will look on those devices.

   ☐ from the upper right of the Preview window, click **Phone Landscape**

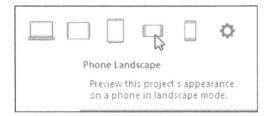

The slide resizes to accommodate a smart phone.

NOTES

Previewing and Storyline Options
Confidence Check

1. Close the Preview window.

2. Select any slide in any scene.

3. Preview the **scene**.

4. Explore the other Responsive Playback options (Tablet Portrait, Phone Portrait).

5. Close the Preview window when finished.

6. Open any slide in any scene and then Preview just the slide.

7. Close the Preview window when finished.

8. Close the slide.

   You've just about wrapped up your initial Storyline tour. Before moving on to the next module (where you'll create the Chesapeake Stables project from scratch), there are some additional Storyline options you should explore.

9. Choose **File > Storyline Options**.

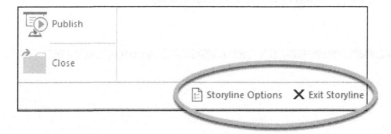

10. From the list at the left, click **General**.

11. Click the **Reset "Don't Show Again Prompts"** button.

12. Click the **OK** button.

    There are several dialog boxes in Storyline that ask you to confirm your action (as shown in the image below). Those dialog boxes may contain the option **Don't ask again**. If you accidentally clicked **Don't ask again**, resetting the option is a great idea.

13. Click the **Spelling Options** button and, at the bottom of the dialog box, click the **Restore Defaults** button. The default Spelling Options will be selected in the Spelling Options dialog box.

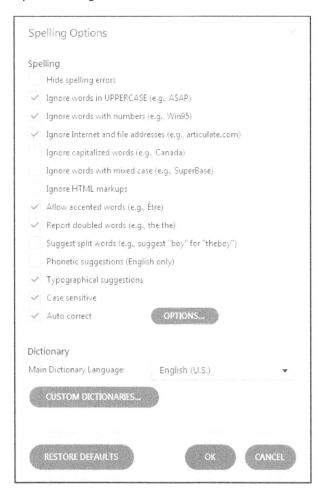

14. Click the **OK** button to close the Spelling Options.

15. From the list at the left, click **Features**.

16. Ensure that **Use the new trigger workflow** is selected.

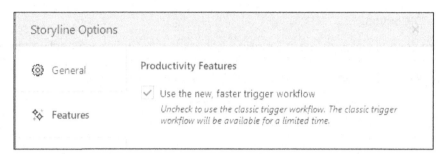

You'll learn about triggers soon. The new trigger workflow makes working with triggers faster and more efficient. However, if you're an experienced developer, you might prefer the Classic workflow. In that case, you would remove the checkmark from "Use the new trigger workflow." For this book, ensure that the option is enabled.

17. Click the **Cancel** button to close the Storyline Options dialog box.

18. Close the project without saving.

iCONLOGiC

"Skills and Drills" Learning

Module 2: Creating Projects

In This Module You Will Learn About:

- Scenes, page 28
- Themes, page 33
- Master Slides, page 34
- Content Slides, page 37

And You Will Learn To:

- Create a New Storyline Project, page 28
- Apply a Theme, page 33
- Apply a Content Master Slide, page 34
- Insert Slides, page 37
- Create a New Content Master Slide, page 39
- Apply a Master Slide Layout to a Slide, page 42

Scenes

A scene is a collection of related slides. Every Storyline project has at least one scene, and you can insert as many scenes as you need. Here's one example where multiple scenes are appropriate: you create a soft skills course about On-boarding and you need to include a quiz. The bulk of the content/slides can be contained in one scene, the quiz in another.

The project you are creating introduces horse owners to a boarding facility named Chesapeake Stables. The finished project will contain seven scenes: Welcome, Farm Culture, Facilities and Options, Riding Lessons, Horse Care Clinic, Quiz, and Videos.

Guided Activity 6: Create a New Storyline Project

1. Ensure Storyline 360 is running.

2. Create a new project.

   ☐ at the left of the Storyline **Welcome** screen, click **New Project**

A new Storyline project is created. By default, you are taken to **Story View**. There is one scene containing one slide.

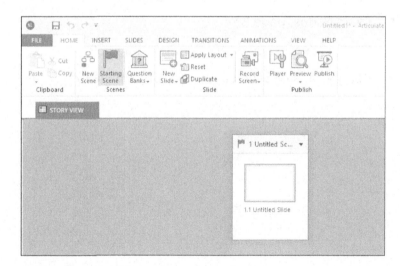

By default, the size of the new project (width and height) is 720 pixels wide by 540 pixels tall (that's an aspect ratio of 4:3, meaning that there are four pixels in height for every three pixels in width).

There is nothing wrong with the default project size if your learners are using devices with a 4:3 aspect ratio (meaning, the displays are more of a square than a rectangle). If your learners are using wider screens (typical on modern devices), a 16:9 aspect ratio is more appropriate. You will change the size of the project in the next step.

3. Change the size of the project.

☐ on the **Ribbon**, select the **Design** tab

☐ at the far left of the **Design** tab, click **Story Size**

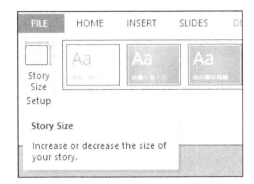

The **Change Story Size** dialog box opens.

☐ from the **Story Size** drop-down menu, choose **720 x 405 (16:9)**

☐ to the right of **Height**, ensure that **Lock aspect ratio** is selected

☐ change the **Width** to **850**

☐ click in the **Height** field

Notice that the **Height** automatically changes to **478** because 850 x 478 is a 16:9 aspect ratio.

Change for mine – answer to why pink background.

☐ click the **OK** button

NOTES

4. Create a new scene.

   ☐ on the **Ribbon**, select the **Home** tab

   ☐ from the **Scenes** group, click **New Scene**

A second scene is added to Story View at the right of the first scene.

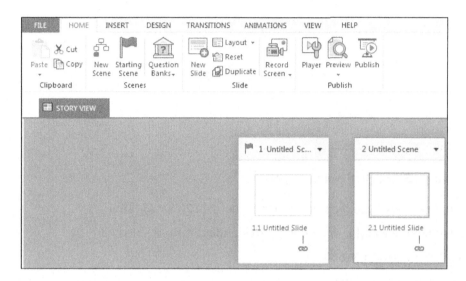

5. Create another new scene.

   ☐ on the **Home** tab, **Scenes** group, click **New Scene** again

A third scene is added to Story View.

6. Create a fourth new scene.

   ☐ click **New Scene** again

A fourth scene is added. All of the scenes you have added are Untitled. Notice that Scene 1 has a red flag in the upper left corner.

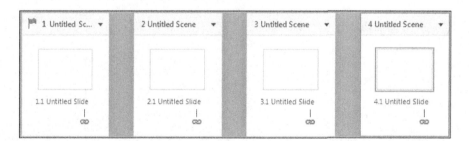

The red flag indicates a project's **Starting Scene** (the first scene displayed when you preview the project). Any scene can be designated as the Starting Scene by first selecting the scene and then choosing **Home > Scenes > Starting Scene**.

7. Add and delete a scene.

   ☐ on the **Home** tab of the Ribbon, **Scenes** group, click **New Scene**

You should now have five untitled scenes.

❐ working in **Story View**, right-click Scene **5** and choose **Delete**

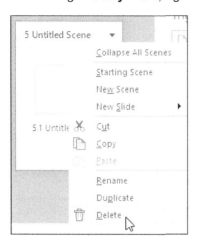

Note: When deleting a scene, ensure that you right-click the scene, **not the slide within the scene**. If you delete a slide within a scene, the scene is not deleted. Also, you can tell that a scene is selected when there is a thin blue outline around the entire scene.

You are prompted to confirm the deletion.

❐ click the **Yes** button

8. Rename a scene.

❐ double-click the first scene's name (where it says "1 Untitled Scene")

❐ replace the existing scene's name with **Welcome** and then press [**enter**]

9. Save the project to the **Storyline360Data_SecondEdition** folder as **Chesapeake-Stables**.

Storyline projects are automatically assigned .**story** extensions.

Scenes Confidence Check

1. Add a new scene.

2. Delete the new scene.

3. Rename each of the three remaining Untitled scenes as follows:

   Scene 2: **Farm Culture**

   Scene 3: **Facilities and Options**

   Scene 4: **Riding Lessons**

4. Create three more scenes and name them:

   Scene 5: **Horse Care Clinic**

   Scene 6: **Quiz**

   Scene 7: **Videos**

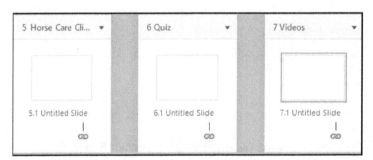

5. Save the project (keep it open for the next activity).

Themes

A theme is a collection of layouts that include positioned slide elements, master and content slides, styled objects, fonts, and colors designed to quickly give a project a consistent look and feel. Similar to Microsoft PowerPoint, Storyline comes with several themes that can be applied project-wide in seconds.

Guided Activity 7: Apply a Theme

1. Ensure that the **Chesapeake-Stables** project is still open.

2. Apply a theme to the project slides.

   ☐ on the **Ribbon**, select the **Design** tab

   Notice that the themes on the Ribbon are grayed out. You cannot apply a theme until you select a slide.

   ☐ select **any slide** in **any scene**

   ☐ at the right of the **Themes** group, click the **More** arrow (shown in the circle below)

   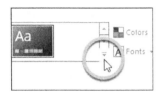

   ☐ select the **Stripes** theme

   All of the project slides now follow the look of the **Stripes** theme. Although you can easily switch from one theme to another, any customization you make to a theme while working on a project is lost when a new theme is applied (such as modifying Master Slides, which you will learn how to do next). It's a best practice to choose a theme early in the development process to avoid extra work later.

3. Apply a different theme to the project slides.

   ☐ select **any slide** in **any scene**

   ☐ at the right of the **Themes** group, click the **More** arrow

   ☐ select the **Trinidad Light** theme

Master Slides

If you need to add common objects to your slides, such as images or background colors, Master Slides are perfect. Each Storyline theme contains one Main Master Slide and multiple Content Master Slides, which are considered children of the Main Master Slide.

Instead of manually copying and pasting common objects onto every slides, you can add common objects to a Master Slide. Then it's a simple matter of applying a Content Master Slide to selected project slides. Any objects on the Content Master Slide appear on the project slides.

Guided Activity 8: Apply a Content Master Slide

1. Ensure that the **Chesapeake-Stables** project is still open.

2. Review the existing slide masters.

    ☐ select the **View** tab on the Ribbon

    ☐ from the **Views** group, click **Slide Master**

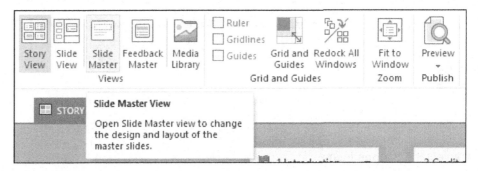

There are six slides at the left of the screen. The first slide is the Main Master slide. The five smaller slides are Content Master Slides. These slides were automatically created when you created the new project. They were formatted when you applied the theme to the project. Later in this module, you will learn how to edit slide masters. For now, you'll leave things as they are and apply a Content Master Slide on an existing slide.

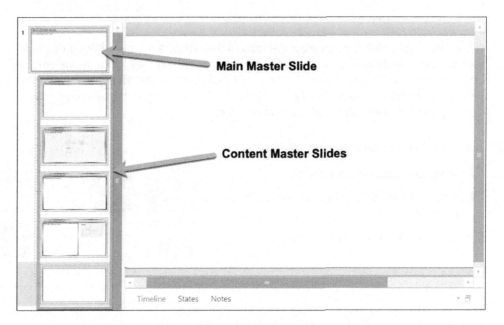

3. Close the Master View.

   ☐ on the **View** tab of the Ribbon, **Close** group, click **Close Master View**

4. Open a slide from within a scene.

   ☐ in the **Welcome** scene, double-click **1.1 Untitled Slide**

   The slide opens in Slide View.

5. Assign the Title Only Content Master Slide to a slide.

   ☐ on the **Home** tab of the Ribbon, **Slide** group, click the **Apply Layout** drop-down menu

   The Content Master Slides for the selected theme open.

   ☐ select the **Title Only** Content Master

   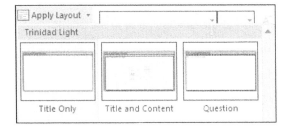

   A Title placeholder is added to the slide.

6. Add a title.

   ☐ with the **Title** placeholder selected, type **A Guide to Our Facilities**
   ☐ click away from the placeholder to deselect it

   Notice that the text you typed within the Title placeholder has automatically updated the slide title in the Scenes window.

   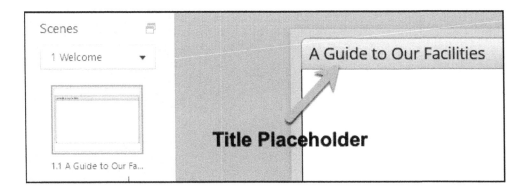

Master Slides Confidence Check

1. Switch to the **Farm Culture** scene.

2. Assign the **Title Only** Content Master Slide to the slide in the **Farm Culture** scene.

3. Title the slide **Family Values and Hard Work**.

4. Switch to the **Facilities and Options** scene.

5. Assign the **Title Only** Content Master Slide to the untitled slide in the scene.

6. Title the slide **Farm Services**.

7. Switch to the **Riding Lessons** scene.

8. Assign the **Title Only** Content Master Slide to the untitled slide in the scene.

9. Title the slide **Equestrian Training for All Ages**.

10. Switch to the **Horse Care Clinic** scene.

11. Assign the **Title Only** Content Master Slide to the untitled slide in the scene.

12. Title the slide **Horse Care Clinic**.

13. Switch to the **Quiz** scene.

14. Assign the **Title Only** Content Master Slide to the untitled slide in the scene.

15. Title the slide **Test Your Knowledge**.

16. Switch to the **Videos** scene.

17. Assign the **Title Only** Content Master Slide to the untitled slide in the scene.

18. Title the slide **Side-Saddle Clinic**.

19. Save and close the project.

Content Slides

Content slides are the backbone of most Storyline projects. The content slides you add to your project can be created from scratch in Storyline, imported from other Storyline projects, or imported PowerPoint presentations. During the following activity, you'll create content slides from scratch. Later (page 46), you'll import content from an existing PowerPoint presentation.

Guided Activity 9: Insert Slides

1. Open the **SlideMe** project from the Storyline360Data_SecondEdition folder.

   Have you forgotten how to open a Storyline project? Here's a hint: look for the **Browse for more** link at the bottom left of the Welcome screen.

2. Insert a new slide.

   ☐ on the **Welcome** scene, open slide **1.1 A Guide to Our Facilities**

   ☐ on the **Ribbon**, select the **Slides** tab and, in the **Slide** group, click the **little menu** at the bottom right of the **New Slide** icon (the menu is shown circled below)

   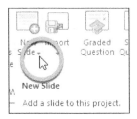

   The Theme being used in the project is **Trinidad Light**. There are five Content master slides resulting in five different layouts from which to choose.

   ☐ select **Title Only**

   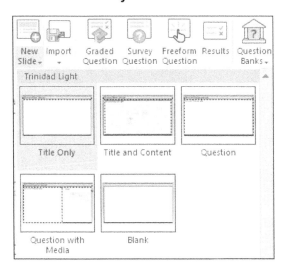

   A second untitled slide is added to the **Welcome** scene.

3. Title the new slide.

☐ on the new slide, replace the title placeholder text with **It's All About You** and then click away from the text

The title you added appears both on the slide and on the Scenes window.

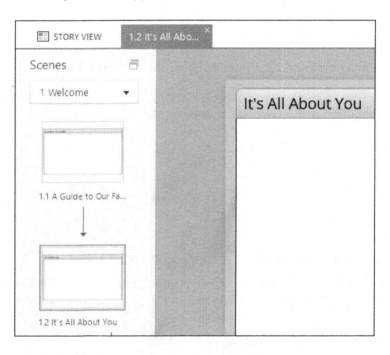

4. Save the project.

Guided Activity 10: Create a New Content Master Slide

1. Ensure that the **SlideMe** project is still open and in **Story View**.

2. Create a new Content Master slide.

   ☐ on the **Ribbon**, select the **View** tab

   ☐ from the **Views** group, click **Slide Master**

   A new tab appears on the Ribbon: **Slide Master**. Notice (confirm) that the second slide in the list is highlighted.

   ☐ on the **Slide Master** tab, **Edit Master** group, click **Insert Layout**

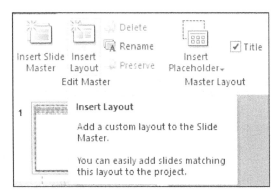

A custom layout is added to the list of layouts at the left. Because the second layout was selected *before* you inserted the new layout, the new layout slide is the **third** slide from the top (new layouts are always added after selected layouts). If you hover over the third slide from the top, you will see that it's named **Layout 'Custom' used by no slides**.

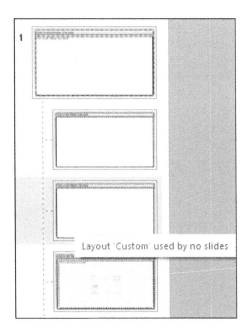

3. Insert a Placeholder onto a Layout.

☐ ensure that you're working on the Custom layout (the third slide from the top)

☐ on the **Slide Master** tab, **Master Layout** group, click the **bottom portion** of **Insert Placeholder**

☐ choose **Text**

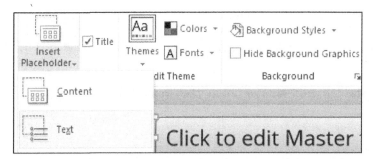

Notice that your mouse pointer becomes a cross when you place your mouse pointer within the body of the slide. You can now drag to create a text box.

☐ drag to create a text box that looks similar to the image below

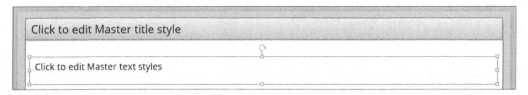

4. Change the name of the Content Master Slide.

☐ at the left of the window, right-click the Custom layout and choose **Rename Layout**

The Rename dialog box opens.

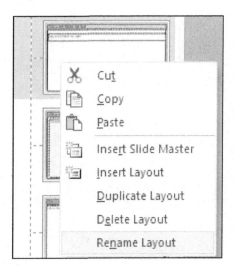

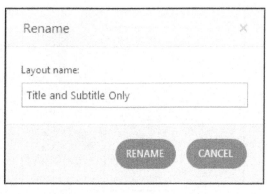

☐ change the name from **Custom** to **Title and Subtitle Only**

☐ click the **Rename** button

5. Close the Master View.

☐ on the **Slide Master** tab of the Ribbon, click **Close Master View**

Guided Activity 11: Apply a Master Slide Layout to a Slide

1. Ensure that the **SlideMe** project is still open and in Story View.

2. Apply a layout to slide.

   ☐ open slide **1.2 It's All About You**

   ☐ on the **Scenes** window, right-click slide **1.2** and choose **Apply Layout > Title and Subtitle Only**

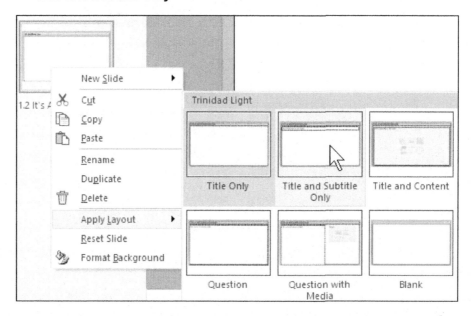

3. Replace the placeholder text.

   ☐ replace the text in the placeholder with **Enter your name and press continue**

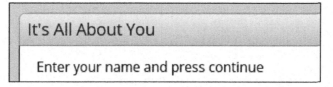

4. Close slide 1.2 to return to Story View.

Content Confidence Check

1. Still working in the **SlideMe** project, open the Farm Culture scene.

2. Add a new slide that uses the **Title Only** layout.

3. Change the title on slide 2.2 to **Instilling Hard Work & Values.**

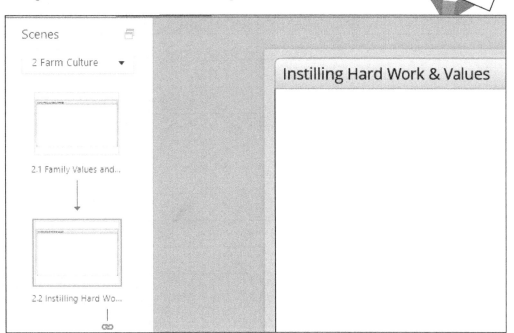

4. Save your work and close the project.

Notes

iCONLOGiC

"Skills and Drills" Learning

Module 3: Adding Content

In This Module You Will Learn About:

And You Will Learn To:

PowerPoint Integration

If you have already created a presentation using Microsoft PowerPoint and want to use that content for eLearning, there's no need to recreate that content in Storyline. You can import the presentation slides into an existing Storyline project or create a new project that uses the PowerPoint slides. Once you have imported the PowerPoint slides into Storyline, most of the PowerPoint objects can be moved or edited directly within Storyline.

> **Note:** You must have PowerPoint 2007 or newer installed on your computer before you can import PowerPoint content into Articulate Storyline.

Guided Activity 12: Import Content From PowerPoint

1. Open the **PowerPointMe** project from the **Storyline360Data_SecondEdition** folder.

2. Import a slide from an existing PowerPoint presentation into a new Storyline scene.

   ❑ on the **Ribbon**, click the **Slides** tab

   ❑ from the **Slide** group, choose
   Import > **Import PowerPoint**

   ❑ from the **Storyline360Data_Second
   Edition** folder, open
   PowerPointContent.pptx

   A preview of the slide in the
   PowerPointContent Presentation appears.

   ❑ from the **Insert into scene** drop-down menu, ensure **New scene** is selected

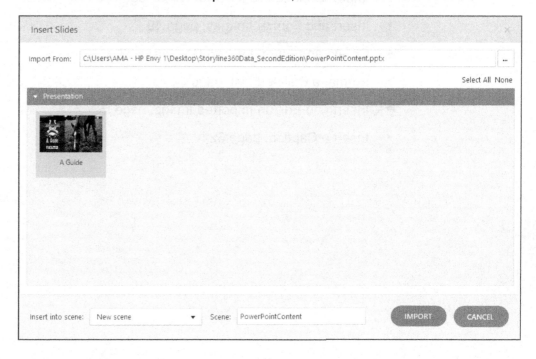

   ❑ click the **Import** button

   The PowerPoint slide is imported into a new Storyline scene called **PowerPointContent**.

---

3. Move a slide into a different scene.

   ☐ from the **PowerPointContent** scene, drag the slide into Scene 1 (Welcome) **just above slide 1.1**

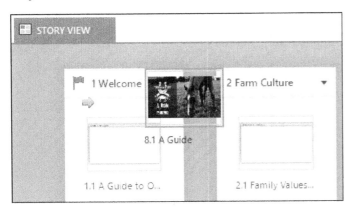

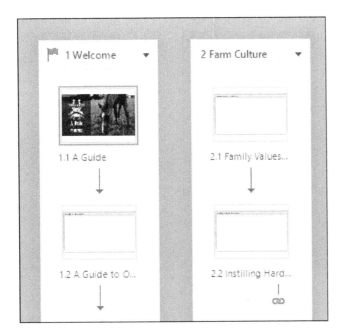

4. Review the imported PowerPoint slide.

   ☐ open slide **1.1 A Guide**

   The PowerPoint slide, text, and two images imported nicely into Storyline.

   ☐ at the bottom of the Storyline window, click **Notes**

   The text that was added to the Notes area in PowerPoint appears in the Storyline Notes area. This text will be used as the slide's voiceover script later.

Welcome to Chesapeake Stables. We offer exceptional care for the horse and rider of every discipline. Click the Start button to take a tour of our facilities and learn about our services.

PowerPoint Confidence Check

1. Still working in the **PowerPointMe** project, delete slide **1.2 A Guide to Our Facilities** (because you've imported the content from PowerPoint, this slide is no longer needed).

2. Rename slide 1.1 as **A Guide to Our Facilities**.

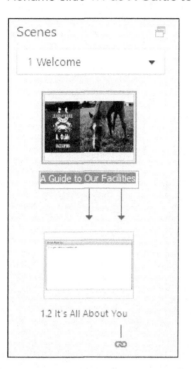

3. Go to the **Slide Master** View.

   Scroll down and notice that the master slides used in the PowerPoint presentation have been imported into the Storyline project. (You learned how to access Master View beginning on page 34.)

4. Close the Master View.

5. Close the slide to return to Story View.

6. Delete **Scene 8 PowerPointContent**.

   Because you've moved the only slide in Scene 8 to Scene 1, Scene 8 is no longer needed.

7. Save and close the project.

Images

Storyline lets you import several graphic formats onto a slide including, but not limited to, **BMP** (Windows Bitmaps), **GIF** (Graphics Interchange Format), **JPG** or **JPEG** (Joint Photographic Expert Group), and **PNG** (Portable Network Graphics).

Guided Activity 13: Insert and Format Images

1. Open the **ContentMe** project from the Storyline360Data_SecondEdition folder.

2. Insert an image.

   ☐ open slide **2.2 Hard Work and Values**

   ☐ select the **Insert** tab on the **Ribbon**

   ☐ from the **Media** group, click the drop-drown menu beneath **Picture** and choose **Picture from File**

   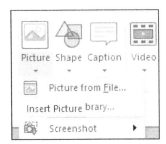

   ☐ from **Storyline360Data_SecondEdition > images_videos**, open **responsibility.png**

   ☐ drag the image a few inches to the left (to leave space for another image)

   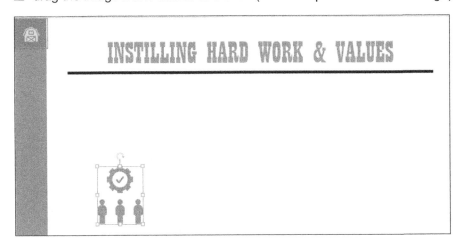

3. Insert another image.

   ☐ ensure that you're still working on slide **2.2 Hard Work and Values**

   ☐ select the **Insert** tab on the **Ribbon**

   ☐ from the **Media** group, click the drop-drown menu beneath **Picture** and choose **Picture from File**

   ☐ from **Storyline360Data_SecondEdition > images_videos**, open **timemanagement.png**

The new image is a bit too large. You'll resize it next.

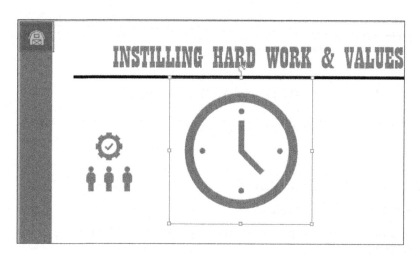

4. Resize the image proportionally.

❑ position your mouse pointer on any one of the image's **corners** (the corners are referred to as **resizing handles**)

❑ drag a corner resizing handle inward to make the image smaller proportionally

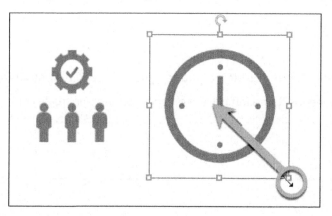

5. Use the Size and Position dialog box to resize an image.

❑ right-click the image you just resized and choose **Size and Position**

The Size and Position dialog box opens.

❑ from the left side of the dialog box, select **Size**

❑ from the **Size and rotate** area, change the Height to **130**

❑ ensure that the Width is also **130**

❑ click the **Close** button

Images Confidence Check

1. Still working on slide **2.2** of the **ContentMe** project, insert the **teamwork** image onto the slide (the image is in the **images_videos** folder).

2. Resize the image approximately the same size as the other two slide images.

3. Insert **notroublehorse** image onto slide **2.2 Hard Work and Values**.

4. Resize the image approximately the same size as the other images.

5. Position the images similar to the picture shown below.

6. Save your work.

Text Boxes

Text can be inserted onto any Storyline slide by typing directly into text boxes, shapes, or captions. You can also copy and paste text from existing sources, such as your favorite word processor, website, or email.

Guided Activity 14: Create and Format a Text Box

1. Ensure that the **ContentMe** project is still open.

2. Ensure that slide **2.2 Hard Work and Values** is still open.

3. Insert a Text Box and add content to it.

    ☐ select the **Insert** tab on the **Ribbon**

    ☐ from the **Text** group, click **Text Box**

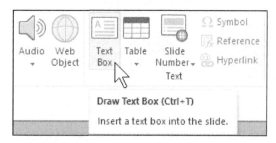

Your mouse pointer changes appearance and is now a cross, an indicator that you can draw an object.

☐ draw a small box beneath the image at the far left

☐ type **Teaches Responsibility**

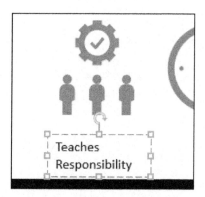

4. Format text.

    ☐ click the border surrounding the text box

    ☐ select the **Home** tab on the **Ribbon**

    ☐ from the **Font** group, change the **Font size** to **14**

    ☐ from the **Font** group, change the **Style** to **Bold** by clicking the letter **B**.

    ☐ from the **Paragraph** group, change the **Alignment** to **Center**

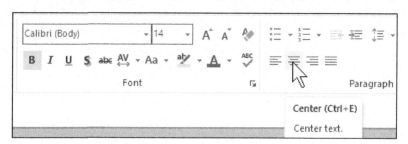

Text Boxes Confidence Check

1. Still working on slide **2.2 Hard Work and Values**, insert three more text boxes

   Box 2 below the clock: **Improves Time Management Skills**

   Box 3 below the hands: **Fosters Teamwork**

   Box 4 below the horse: **Keeps Kids Out of Trouble**

2. Format the text in each of the new boxes as Calibri, 14 point, Bold, and Centered.

3. Resize and position each of the text boxes similar to the image shown below.

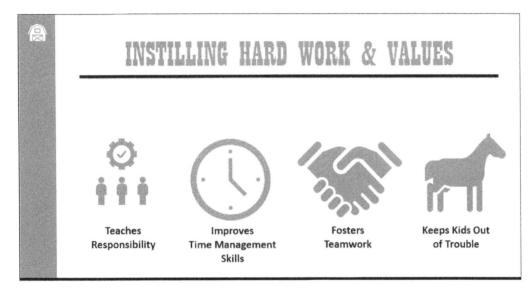

4. Save your work and keep the project open.

Guided Activity 15: Format a Bulleted List

1. Ensure that the **ContentMe** project is still open.

2. Copy and paste content from MS Word onto a Storyline slide.

   ☐ start **Microsoft Word**

   ☐ using **Word**, open the **Chesapeake_Stables_Storyboard** document from the **Storyline360Data_SecondEdition** folder

   ☐ scroll down to the **Scene 3, Slide 3.2** section of the document.

   ☐ in the left column, select all of the text beneath the phrase *Right side text:*

Slide: 3.2	*Title: Facilities Overview*
On-Screen	Narration
Top Notch Stable Facilities Right-side text: Among the many amenities you'll enjoy at Chesapeake Stables are: Bright, airy stalls. A large indoor arena for riding and lessons no matter the weather. 10-acres of well-maintained pastures, and a portable hot water shower system to ensure ultimate comfort for your horse. There is also on-site vehicle and trailer parking.	Among the many amenities you'll enjoy at Chesapeake Stables are bright, airy stalls, a large indoor arena for riding and lessons no matter the weather, 10-acres of well-maintained pastures, and a portable hot water shower system to ensure ultimate comfort for your horse. There is also on-site vehicle and trailer parking.

   ☐ copy the text ([**ctrl**] [**c**] works great)

3. Return to Storyline and ensure that the **ContentMe** project is still open.

4. Paste content from Word into Storyline.

   ☐ open slide **3.2**

   ☐ click inside the text placeholder where you see the words **Click to add text**

   ☐ right-click within the text placeholder and, from the **Paste Options** area, choose **Use Destination Theme**

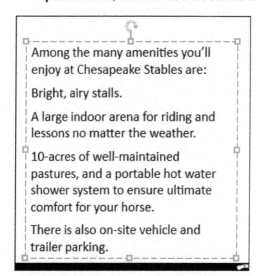

Among the many amenities you'll enjoy at Chesapeake Stables are:

Bright, airy stalls.

A large indoor arena for riding and lessons no matter the weather.

10-acres of well-maintained pastures, and a portable hot water shower system to ensure ultimate comfort for your horse.

There is also on-site vehicle and trailer parking.

5. Add a bulleted list.

❑ highlight all of the text within the text box except the heading "Among the many amenities you'll enjoy at Chesapeake Stables are:"

❑ click the **Home** tab on the Ribbon

❑ from the **Paragraph** group, click the drop-down menu to the right of **Bullets**

❑ click the **cubes** bullet

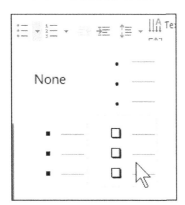

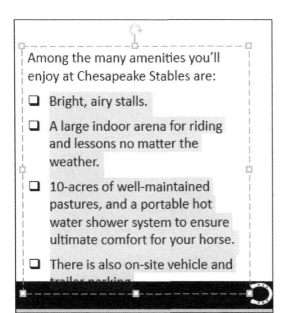

Text Formatting Confidence Check

Notice that the bulleted list is a bit too deep and runs off of the page into the black bar. You'll use Storyline's **Spacing After** options to reduce the space between the bullets and fix the problem.

1. With the bulleted text selected, go to the **Format** tab on the Ribbon > **Line Spacing** and choose **Line Spacing Options.**

2. Change the **Spacing After** to **0**.

Spacing	
Before:	0 pt
After:	0 pt

3. Click the **OK** button.

   With less spacing between the paragraphs, the bulleted list now fits nicely on the page.

4. Save your work.

The Content Library

Included with the Articulate 360 subscription is access to millions of course assets, such as photos, illustrations, videos, slide templates, interactions, characters, and icons. You can insert any of the assets found in the Content Library directly from within Storyline via the Insert tab on the Ribbon. Many of the assets can be edited directly from within Storyline (for instance, you can change an image from color to black and white, and add other visual effects).

Guided Activity 16: Insert and Edit an Imported Image

1. Ensure that the **ContentMe** project is still open.

2. Insert a horse image from the Content Library.

   ❑ go to Story View open slide **5.2 Long in the Tooth**

   ❑ select the **Insert** tab on the Ribbon

   ❑ from the **Content Library 360** group, click **Photos**

   The Search Photos dialog box opens.

   ❑ type **horse teeth** into the search area and press [**enter**] to search

   ❑ select the image shown below at the right

   Note: If the image shown below does not appear when you Search (perhaps you're offline or Articulate deleted the image from the Library), you can Insert the **horse_teeth** image from the **Storyline360Data_SecondEdition > images_videos** folder.

   ❑ click the **Insert** button

   The image appears in the middle of the slide.

3. Change the color of an image to black and white.

   ❑ still working on slide **5.2**, select the horse image you imported from the Content Library

NOTES

☐ select the **Picture Tools** tab on the Ribbon

☐ at the left of the **Format** tab, **Adjust** group, click **Recolor** and choose **Accent color 3 Dark**

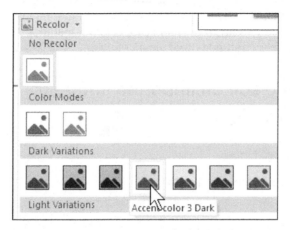

4. Crop an image.

☐ still working on slide **5.2**, select the horse image

☐ at the right of the **Picture Tools** tab, **Size and Position** group, click the **Crop** tool

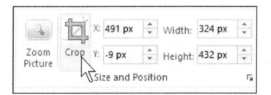

☐ drag the **upper left** cropping handle diagonally down toward the horse similar to the image below

❏ drag the bottom right cropping handle diagonally up toward the horse's jaw

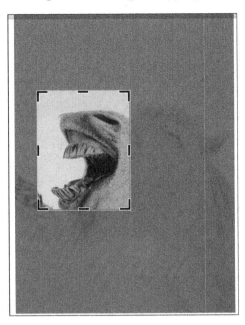

❏ press [**escape**] on your keyboard to finish the cropping process

5. Resize the image.

❏ still working on slide **5.2**, ensure that the cropped horse image is still selected

❏ drag the horse image up and to the left until your slide is similar to the image below, at the left

❏ on the horse image, select the **bottom right** resizing handle and drag it **down and to the right** to make the image about three times larger than its current size

NOTES

Cropping and Resizing Confidence Check

1. Still working on slide **5.2**, **resize**, **move**, and **re-crop** the horse image to make your slide similar to the image below.

2. Open slide **5.3**.

3. Search the **Content Library** Photos for **horse hoof** and insert the image shown below onto the slide. (If you cannot find the image in the Content Library, insert the **horse_hoof** image manually from the images_video folder).

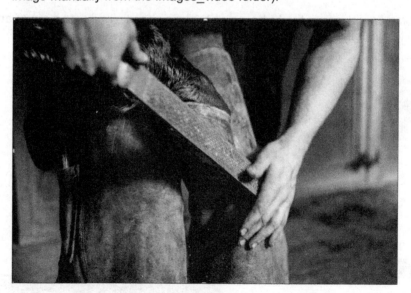

4. Change the color of the image to **Accent color 3 Dark**.

5. Resize, crop, and position the image as shown in the image below.

6. Select the **View** tab on the Ribbon and click **Media Library**.

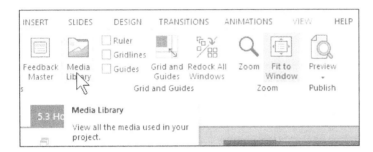

All of the project's assets (Images, Characters, Audio) are stored in the Media Library. You can use the Library to add the assets to any slide again or replace assets project-wide. (You'll get a chance to replace media assets during an activity on page 176.)

7. Close the Media Library.

8. Save your work.

Captions

Captions are similar to Shapes, but they contain pointers that indicate speech or thoughts. You can add text to Captions and format them like any other Shape.

Guided Activity 17: Insert a Caption

1. Ensure that the **ContentMe** project is still open.

2. Insert a Caption.

   ☐ open slide 5.2

   ☐ select the **Insert** tab on the **Ribbon**

   ☐ from the **Media** group, click **Caption**

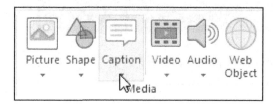

   ☐ select the **Oval Caption**

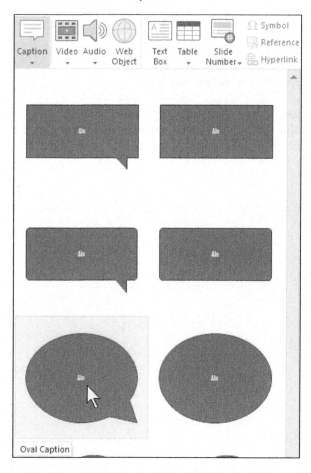

   ☐ draw a caption on the slide just above and to the left of the horse's top teeth

❏ with the caption selected, type **Look at my Galvayne's groove.**

❏ select the caption text and, using the **Home** tab on the Ribbon, change the Font and Font size as you see fit

❏ on the caption, drag the **yellow square** toward the next to the last top tooth as shown in the image below

3. Save and close the project.

Notes

iCONLOGiC

"Skills and Drills" Learning

Module 4: Buttons, Triggers, and Hotspots

In This Module You Will Learn About:

- Buttons and Triggers, page 66
- Hotspots, page 79

And You Will Learn To:

- Add Button to a Slide, page 66
- Add a Trigger to a Button, page 68
- Use an Image as a Button, page 71
- Edit a Trigger, page 73
- Remove Default Player Buttons, page 76
- Make a Slide Advance Automatically, page 78
- Insert a Hotspot, page 79

NOTES

Buttons and Triggers

Buttons are arguably the most common type of interactive objects you'll see in Storyline projects. Using triggers, you can control what happens when a learner successfully click a button. Common triggers include, but are not limited to, jumping to a different slide, playing audio, showing a layer, playing an animation, and more.

Guided Activity 18: Add Button to a Slide

1. Open **ButtonHotspotMe** from the Storyline360Data_SecondEdition folder.

2. Insert a button onto a slide.

   ☐ open slide **1.1 A Guide to Our Facilities**

   ☐ select the **Insert** tab on the Ribbon

   ☐ from the **Interactive Objects** group, click **Button**

   ☐ select the **first button type**

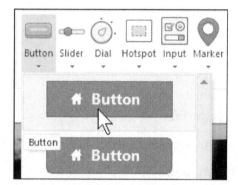

   ☐ on the slide, draw a button

   ☐ type **START** into the button

   ☐ move and resize the button similar to the image below

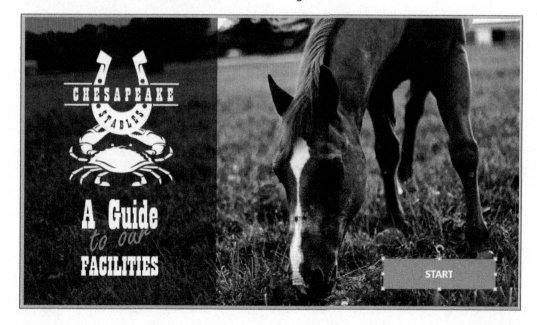

3. Insert an icon into a button.

    ☐ ensure that the button that you drew is selected

    ☐ from the left of the **Button Tools Format** tab on the Ribbon, **Button Icons** group, select any **Button Icon**

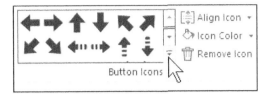

The Button Icon appears in front of the START text that you typed in the button.

Next, you'll give the button a name. As your project gets more complicated and the number of interactive objects increases, naming objects will prove invaluable.

4. Name the button.

    ☐ ensure the button selected

    ☐ on the **Timeline**, double-click the name **Button 1** and replace it with **Start Button**

    ☐ press [**enter**] to activate the new name

At this point, the button is nothing more than a slide object. During the next activity, you'll add a trigger to the button to make it interactive.

5. Save your work.

NOTES

Guided Activity 19: Add a Trigger to a Button

1. Ensure that the **ButtonHotspotMe** project is still open.

2. Add a trigger to a button.

   ☐ ensure that the button is selected

   ☐ on the **Triggers** window at the right of the Storyline screen, click the **Create a new trigger** icon

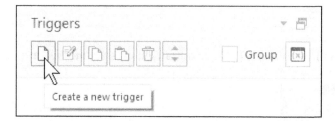

The Trigger Wizard opens.

   ☐ from the **Action** area, ensure that **Jump to slide** is selected

   ☐ from the **Slide** area, ensure that **next slide** is selected

Thanks to the first two options, the learner will end up on slide **1.2 It's All About You**. But when? How? That's where the **When** and **Object** options come into play.

   ☐ from the **When** area, ensure that **When the user clicks** is selected

   ☐ from the **Object** area, ensure that **Start Button** is selected

In summary, this trigger will take the learner to the next slide in the scene *when* the learner clicks the Start Button. Are you curious about the **Conditions** area? You'll explore this feature later.

❏ click the **OK** button

The new trigger is added to the Triggers window in the **Object Triggers** area.

3. Preview the scene.

4. After the preview is generated, click the **Start Button**.

   Thanks to the trigger, clicking the Start Button takes you to Slide **1.2 It's All About You**.

5. Close the Preview.

6. Save the project.

NOTES

Text Button Confidence Check

1. Still working in the **ButtonHotspotMe** project, open slide **1.2**.

2. Insert a button that contains the word **Continue**.

3. Add a **Button Icon** to the button. (**Note:** When adding the Button Icon, if you want the icon to appear on the right side of the button as shown in the first image below, choose **Align Right** from the **Align icon** drop-down menu as shown in the second image below.)

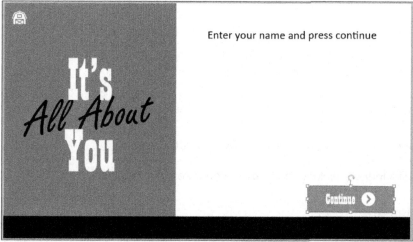

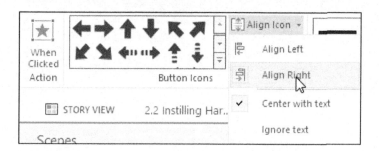

4. On the Timeline, name the button **Continue Button**.

5. Add a new trigger to the **Continue Button** that **Jumps** the learner to the next slide when the **Continue Button** is clicked.

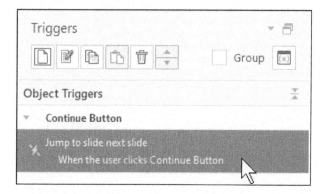

6. Preview the scene and test the buttons you've added.

7. Close the Preview.

Guided Activity 20: Use an Image as a Button

1. Ensure that the **ButtonHotspotMe** project is still open.

2. Make an image an interactive button.

   ☐ open slide **1.3 Welcome** *and* select the **horseshoe image** at the **bottom right corner** of the slide

   On the Timeline, notice that the image is named **Right Shoe**.

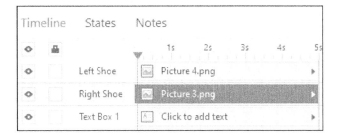

   ☐ on the **Triggers** window, click the **Create a new trigger** icon

   The Trigger Wizard opens.

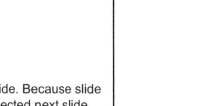

Triggers

Create a new trigger

   ☐ from the **Action** area, ensure that **Jump to slide** is selected

   ☐ from the **Slide** area, select **2.1 Family Values and Hard Work**

   ☐ from the **When** area, ensure that **When the user clicks** is selected

   ☐ from the **Object** area, ensure that **Right Shoe** is selected

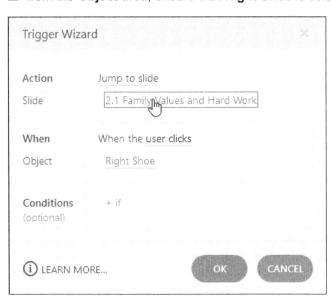

You selected a **specific slide** (2.1) in the step above instead of next slide. Because slide 1.3 is the last slide in the Scene 1, **there is no next slide**. Had you selected next slide, learners who click the horseshoe image on slide 1.3 would not go anywhere.

   ☐ click the **OK** button

NOTES

Image Trigger Confidence Check

1. Select the Left Shoe image and add a trigger that takes the learner to the **previous slide** when the image is clicked.

2. Preview the entire project and test the two horseshoe links on Slide **1.3**.

3. Close the Preview.

4. Still working on Slide **1.3**, select both horseshoe images and copy them to the clipboard.

5. Go to Slide **2.1** and paste the images onto the slide.

   Note: When you copy and paste objects in Storyline, all associated object properties, such as triggers and slide position, are included.

6. Save the project.

Guided Activity 21: Edit a Trigger

1. Ensure that the **ButtonHotspotMe** project is still open.

2. Edit a trigger.

    ☐ on Slide **2.1**, select only the **Right Shoe** image

    ☐ on the **Triggers** window, click the **Edit the selected trigger** icon

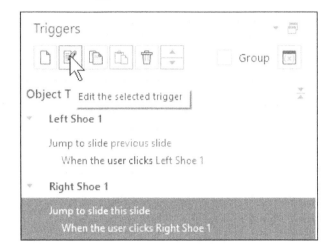

    ☐ from the **Action** area, change the **Slide** to **next slide**

    ☐ click the **OK** button

Editing Triggers Confidence Check

1. On Slide **2.1**, copy **both horseshoe images** to the clipboard.

2. Paste the images onto the following slides:

   ☐ 2.2

   ☐ 3.1

   ☐ 3.2

   ☐ 3.3

   ☐ 4.2

   ☐ 4.3

   ☐ 5.1

   ☐ 5.2

   ☐ 5.3

3. Go to slide **2.2** and edit the trigger for the **right shoe** so that it jumps to slide **3.1 Family Services.**

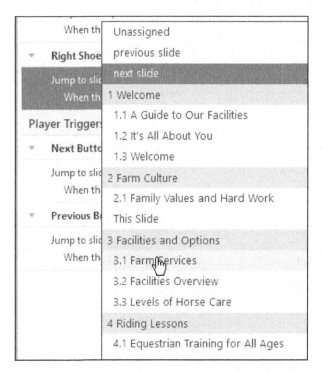

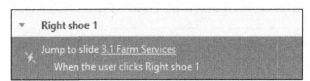

Note: Instead of clicking the **Edit the selected trigger** icon on the Triggers window, you can make the edit using the link directly on the trigger, which is known as **inline editing.**

4. Go to slide **3.3** and edit the trigger for the **right shoe** so that it jumps to slide **4.1**.

---

5. Go to slide **4.3** and edit the trigger for the **right shoe** so that it jumps to slide **5.1**.

6. Save the project.

7. Preview the project.

8. Ensure that your interactive objects work as expected (you should be able to move from slide to slide using the horseshoe navigation you added to most of the slides).

9. On slide **4.1, Equestrian Training for All Ages**, notice that there are no horseshoe images. Instead, the slide contains built-in player buttons in the lower right (shown circled in the image below). By default, these buttons also appear on the other slides.

In the next few activities, you will remove the default player buttons project-wide and configure slide **4.1** so that it moves forward automatically after five seconds.

10. Close the preview.

Guided Activity 22: Remove Default Player Buttons

1. Ensure that the **ButtonHotspotMe** project is still open.

2. Remove the default player buttons for one slide.

   ☐ open slide **1.1**

   ☐ from the lower right of the **Slide Layers** window, click the **Properties** icon

The Slide Properties dialog box opens.

   ☐ from the **Slide navigation and gestures area**, deselect **Prev** and **Next** from both the Buttons and Swipe areas

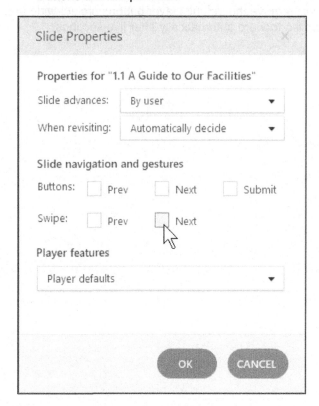

   ☐ click the **OK** button

3. Preview the slide and notice that the default Player buttons have been removed from the slide.

4. Close the preview.

5. Remove the default player buttons from all slides.

   ☐ switch to **Story View**

   ☐ click once on any slide in any scene

   ☐ press [**ctrl**] [**a**] to select all of the slides in the scene

   ☐ press [**ctrl**] [**a**] again to select all of the slides in all of the scenes

   On the Slide Properties window, notice that the **Prev** and **Next** options from both the Buttons and Swipe areas are **blue** indicating that some slides are using the default Player buttons and some are not.

   Slide Properties

   Properties for multiple slides

   Slide advances: By user ▼

   When revisiting: Automatically decide ▼

   Multiple slide navigation and gestures

   Buttons: ▦ Prev   ▦ Next   ☐ Submit

   Swipe: ▦ Prev   ▦ Next

   Player features

   Player defaults ▼

   ☐ from the **Multiple slide navigation and gestures area**, deselect **Prev** and **Next** from both the Buttons and Swipe areas

   Slide Properties

   Properties for multiple slides

   Slide advances: By user ▼

   When revisiting: Automatically decide ▼

   Multiple slide navigation and gestures

   Buttons: ☐ Prev   ☐ Next   ☐ Submit

   Swipe: ☐ Prev   ☐ Next

   Player features

   Player defaults ▼

NOTES

Guided Activity 23: Make a Slide Advance Automatically

1. Ensure that the **ButtonHotspotMe** project is still open.

2. Make a slide advance automatically.

   ☐ still working in Story View, select slide **4.1**

   ☐ on the **Slide Properties** window, **Slide advances** drop-down menu, choose **Automatically**

A trigger is added that tells the slide to Jump to the next slide when the timeline ends (which is five seconds by default). You'll learn more about working with the Timeline later.

3. Preview the entire project.

   Notice that the default player buttons are gone, and when you get to slide 4.1, the slide continues automatically after five seconds.

4. Close the preview.

5. Save your work.

Hotspots

Hotspots are similar to Buttons in that they can be interactive. Unlike Buttons, which are typically visible to the learner on the slide, hotspots are transparent. You insert hotspots over slide assets or areas of a slide and then use triggers to make the hotspot interactive.

Guided Activity 24: Insert a Hotspot

1. Ensure that the **ButtonHotspotMe** project is still open.

2. Insert a hotspot.

   ☐ open slide **5.4**

   ☐ click the **Insert** tab on the Ribbon

   ☐ from the **Interactive Objects** group, click **Hotspot**

   ☐ select the **rectangle shape**

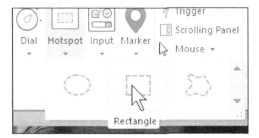

   ☐ on the slide, draw a hotspot shape over the web address for Chesapeake Stables and include the **globe** icon

3. Create a trigger for the hotspot.

   ☐ with the Hotspot selected, click **Create a new trigger** on the **Triggers** window

   ☐ change the **Action** to **Open URL/file**

   Note: The Open URL/file Action is in the **More** group; you'll need to scroll down to find it.

NOTES

❑ in the **File or URL** field, type **https://www.chesapeakestables.com**

❑ press **[enter]**

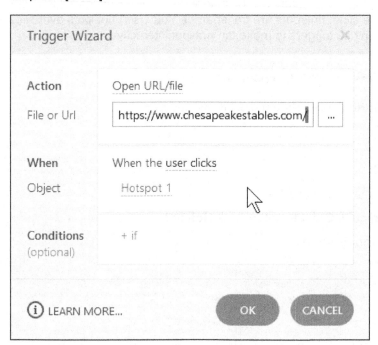

4. Test the URL.

❑ with the Trigger Wizard still open, move your mouse over the web address that you just typed

❑ at the right of the web address, click **Check URL/File**

The Chesapeake Stables website opens. The ability to check the URL from within the Trigger Wizard is a nice feature as you'll discover next.

❑ close the browser window and return to Storyline

❑ click the **OK** button to close the Trigger Wizard

5. Preview slide **5.4** and click the hotspot.

Because links to websites aren't fully functional until you Publish, the link does not work when previewed.

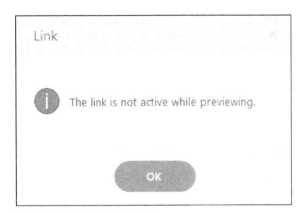

6. Click the OK button on the Link alert.

7. Close the Preview.

8. Save and close the project.

Notes

iCONLOGiC

"Skills and Drills" Learning

Module 5: States, Layers, and Variables

In This Module You Will Learn About:

And You Will Learn To:

States

Every slide object can behave and look differently as the learner interacts with it. For instance, you can assign a Hover State to a button that changes the appearance of the button when the learner hovers above the button, but does not click it. And you can have the button change color when the learner clicks it.

During the next few activities, you'll use the States feature that will change the appearance of slide images as learners interact with them.

Guided Activity 25: Change Button States

1. Open **StateMe** from the Storyline360Data_SecondEdition folder.

2. Open slide **3.3 Levels of Horse Care**.

3. Add a Hover State that makes an image glow when the learner hovers over it with the mouse.

   ❑ on the **Timeline**, select the **image of the grain (grain.png)**

   ❑ from just above the **Timeline**, click **States**

   There is currently one state associated with the selected image called **Normal**.

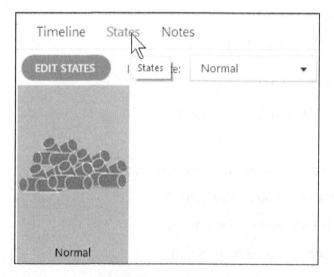

   ❑ click the **Edit States** button

   ❑ click the **New State** icon

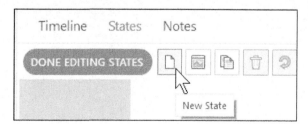

The **Add** dialog box opens.

❑ from the drop-down menu, choose **Hover**

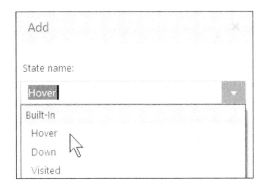

❑ click the **Add** button

The new Hover state is added to the States area.

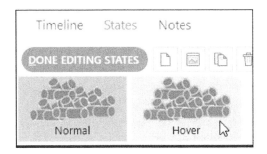

❑ with the new **Hover** state selected, go to the **Format** tab on the **Ribbon**

❑ from the **Picture Effects** drop-down menu choose **Glow > Accent color 2, 24 px glow**

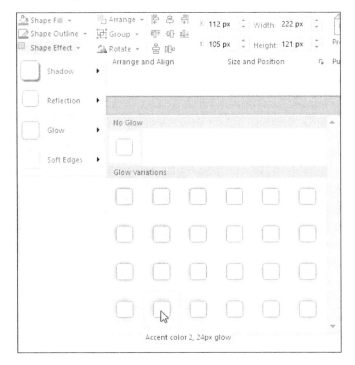

NOTES

4. Finish editing the Hover state.

    ☐ click the **Done Editing States** button

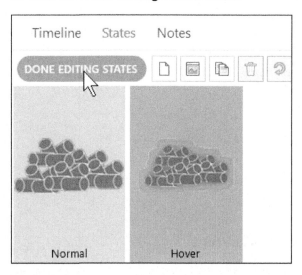

Important! Clicking the **Done Editing States** button is a simple yet crucial step. Should you forget to finish the Editing process and continue editing the slide, those edits become part of the selected State.

5. Save your work.

6. Test the button Hover State using the Preview icons.

    ☐ from the upper right of the Storyline window, click the **Desktop Preview icon**

    ☐ hover your mouse over the image of the grain to see the glow effect

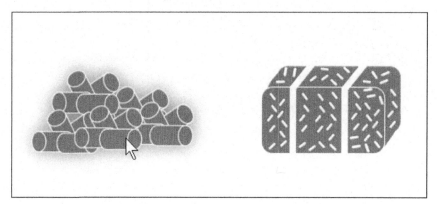

7. Close the Preview.

8. Edit the Hover State by copying and pasting a caption from the pasteboard to the state.

☐ still working on slide **3.3 Levels of Horse Care**, select the **Premium Grain** caption (the caption is located just off the left side of the slide)

☐ **right-click** the caption and choose **Copy**

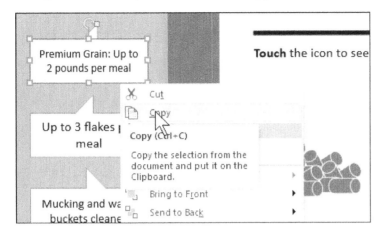

☐ on the slide, select the **grain** image

☐ on the **States** window, click **Edit States**

☐ select the **Hover** state

☐ right-click the slide and choose **Paste**

☐ drag the pasted caption onto the slide and position it just below the image of the grain

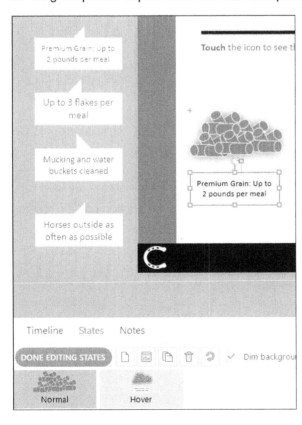

☐ click the **Done Editing States** button

NOTES

States Confidence Check

1. Preview the slide.

   Hover your mouse above the image of the grain to see both the glow effect and the caption text.

Premium Grain: Up to 2 pounds per meal

2. Close the Preview.

3. Add a **Hover** state to the image of the **hay**.

4. While editing the **Hover** state, add the Glow effect and the caption containing the words "Up to 3 flakes...."

5. Preview the slide and test the Hover state for the hay image.

6. Close the Preview window.

7. Add a **Hover** state to the image of the **bucket and rake**.

8. While editing the **Hover** state, add the Glow effect and the caption containing the words "Mucking and water..."

9. Add a **Hover** state to the image of the **fence**.

Up to 3 flakes per meal

10. While editing the **Hover** state, add the Glow effect and the caption containing the words "Horses outside as..."

11. Preview the slide and test the Hover state for all of the images.

12. Close the Preview window.

13. Save and close the project.

Layers

Layers are areas within Storyline that can contain just about any slide object. Because Layers have their own Timeline, they behave much like Storyline slides. By default, new Layers are hidden from learner view. You can use Triggers to control when the hidden Layers appear on a slide. Every new Storyline project contains one Layer, known as the Base Layer. Every object you have added to any of your slides up to this point have all been added to the Base layer.

Guided Activity 26: Create Layers

1. Open the **Finished_Chesapeake_Stables_Project** file from the Storyline360Data_SecondEdition folder.

2. Open slide **4.2 Lesson Varieties**.

3. Preview the slide and click the slide buttons one-by-one: Western, English and Side-Saddle.

    As you click each of the buttons, notice that previously hidden content appears onscreen. The content you see has been added to layers, and each button is triggering the appearance of an individual layer. During this activity you'll learn how to add the layers and the interactivity.

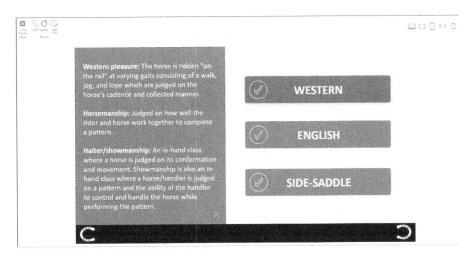

4. Close the preview

5. Close the project.

6. Open the **LayerMe** project from the Storyline360Data_SecondEdition folder.

NOTES

7. Open slide **4.2 Lesson Varieties**.

Notice that there is a **Slide Layers** window at the bottom right of the Storyline screen.

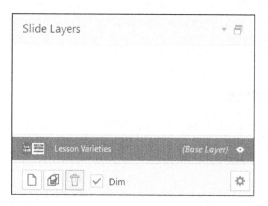

As mentioned above, every Storyline project contains a single layer by default called **Base Layer**. All slide objects are automatically added to the Base Layer.

8. Create a new layer.

☐ from the **bottom** of the **Slide Layers** window, click the **New Layer** icon

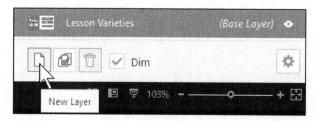

The new layer opens containing the objects from the Base Layer. Notice that the objects from the Base Layer are dimmed in color which means they cannot be edited.

9. Name the new layer.

☐ on the **Slide Layers** window, double-click the name **Untitled Layer 1** and change the name to **Western** and press **[enter]**

10. Cut and paste content from the base layer to the Western layer.

    ☐ on the **Slide Layers** window, click the **Base Layer** (Lesson Varieties)

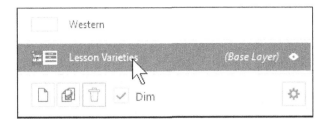

    ☐ on the pasteboard, select **both** the **large x** and the **blue text box**

    ☐ **cut** both objects to the clipboard
    ☐ on the **Slide Layers** window, click the **Western** Layer
    ☐ **paste** the clipboard objects onto the layer

NOTES

☐ drag the pasted objects onto the layer so they cover the **Varieties of Lessons** area on the slide

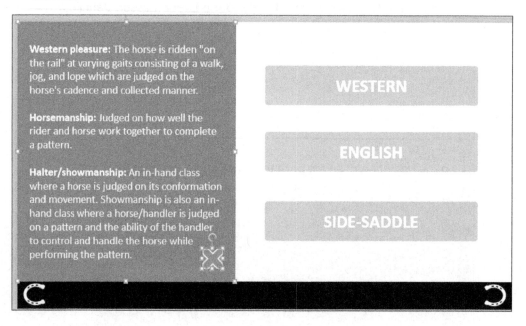

11. Duplicate a layer

☐ on the **Slide Layers** window, right-click the **Western Layer** and choose **Duplicate**

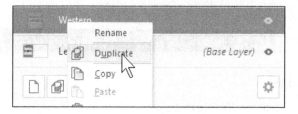

☐ on the **Slide Layers** window, double-click the name **Western-Copy**

☐ change the name of the layer to **English** and then press [**enter**]

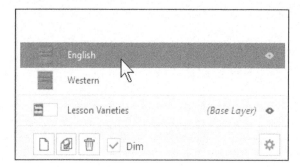

12. Copy and paste content from the Notes window into a layer.

☐ from the bottom of the Storyline window, click **Notes**

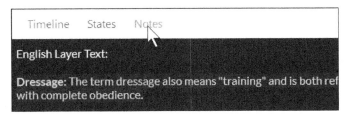

☐ from the **Notes** window, select all of the **English Layer** text (**Dressage** through **Hunt Seat**) and **copy** it to the clipboard

13. Replace text.

☐ in the **English** layer, select all the text in the blue box and replace it with the English Layer text you copied from the Notes panel

Dressage: The term dressage also means "training" and is both referred to a type of training and a type of competition. The emphasis is on natural training to help them perform quietly and calmly with complete obedience.

Hunt Seat: A general term that encompasses any type of forward seat riding.

NOTES

Layers Confidence Check

1. Duplicate the English Layer.

2. Rename the new layer Side-Saddle.

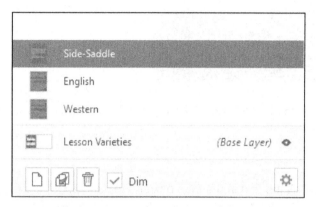

3. Copy the **Side-Saddle text** from the **Notes** window and paste it into the text box on the **Side-Saddle layer**.

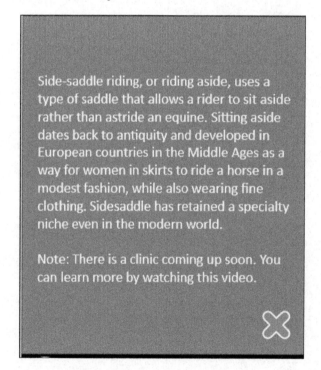

Side-saddle riding, or riding aside, uses a type of saddle that allows a rider to sit aside rather than astride an equine. Sitting aside dates back to antiquity and developed in European countries in the Middle Ages as a way for women in skirts to ride a horse in a modest fashion, while also wearing fine clothing. Sidesaddle has retained a specialty niche even in the modern world.

Note: There is a clinic coming up soon. You can learn more by watching this video.

4. On the **Slide Layers** window, click the **Base Layer (Lesson Varieties)**.

5. Preview the slide.

6. Click any of the buttons on the slide.

Although the buttons change appearance (thanks to different states, which you learned about earlier in this module), information about the riding disciplines does not appear.

You've created layers with information about the different riding disciplines, but layers are hidden from learner view by default. In the next activity, you'll learn how to use triggers to make the hidden layers appear when learners click the appropriate button.

Guided Activity 27: Create a Trigger to Show a Layer

1. Ensure that the **LayerMe** project is still open.

2. Ensure that you're working on the **Base Layer (Lesson Varieties)**.

3. Create a trigger for the **Western** button that will display the Western layer.

   ☐ on the **Timeline**, select **Western Button 1**

   ☐ on the **Triggers** window, click the **Create a new trigger** icon

   ☐ from the **Action** area, choose **Show layer**

   ☐ from the **Layer** area, choose **Western**

   ☐ from the **When** area, ensure **When the user clicks** is selected

   ☐ from the **Object** area, ensure **Western Button 1** is selected

   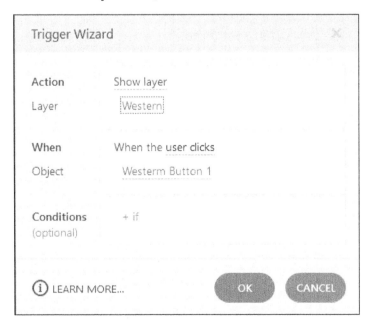

   ☐ click the **OK** button

NOTES

The new trigger appears on the Triggers window.

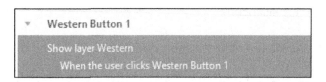

▼   Western Button 1

    Show layer Western
        When the user clicks Western Button 1

4. Preview the slide.

5. Click the Western button on the slide to display the Western layer and its corresponding content.

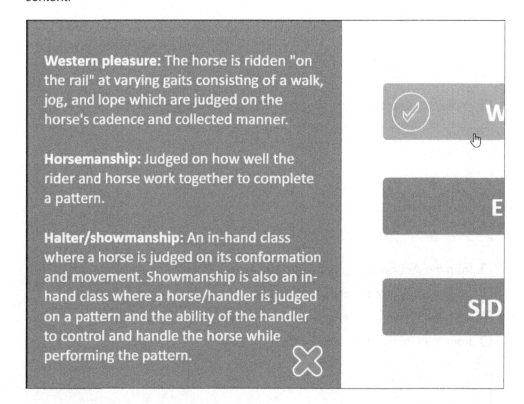

Western pleasure: The horse is ridden "on the rail" at varying gaits consisting of a walk, jog, and lope which are judged on the horse's cadence and collected manner.

Horsemanship: Judged on how well the rider and horse work together to complete a pattern.

Halter/showmanship: An in-hand class where a horse is judged on its conformation and movement. Showmanship is also an in-hand class where a horse/handler is judged on a pattern and the ability of the handler to control and handle the horse while performing the pattern.

6. Close the Preview.

Triggers and Layers Confidence Check

1. Add a trigger for the English button that shows the English layer.

2. Add a trigger for the Side-Saddle button that shows the Side-Saddle layer.

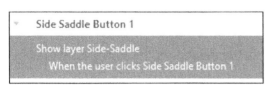

3. Preview the slide and test all three buttons to ensure the corresponding layer displays.

4. Close the Preview.

   Next you'll add a trigger that hides a layer when learners click the close icon (the large X).

5. Open the **Western** layer.

6. Select the **close icon** (the **large X**).

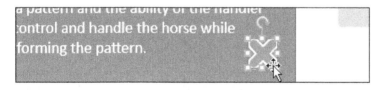

7. Add a trigger to the **close icon** that will **Hide this layer**.

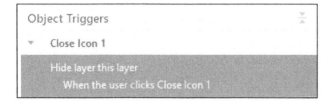

8. Preview the slide, click the **Western** button to show the Western layer.

9. Click the **close icon** to close the Western layer.

10. Close the preview.

11. Ensure that you're still on the **Western** layer.

This provides a way to go back to 1st layer info.

NOTES

12. On the **Triggers** window, select the **Hide layer this layer** trigger you created a moment ago.

13. Click the **Copy the selected trigger** icon at the top of the Triggers window.

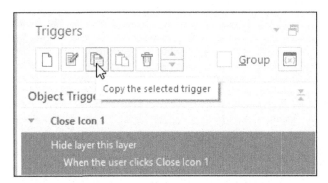

14. Open the **English** layer.

15. Select the **close icon**.

16. On the Triggers window, click the **Paste the copied trigger to the selected object** icon.

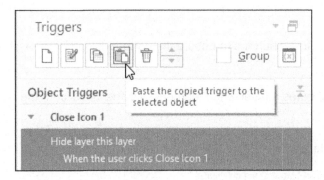

17. Open the **Side-Saddle** layer.

18. Select the **close icon**.

19. On the Triggers window, click the **Paste the copied trigger to the selected object** icon.

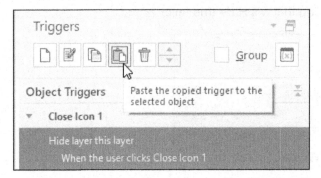

20. Preview the slide, click the buttons to show the appropriate layer, and click the close icon to hide each layer.

21. Close the preview.

22. Save and close the project.

Text Entry Fields

Text Entry Fields allow a learner to type data directly onto your slides. Learners can be instructed to type something specific or be allowed to type anything they like. Once a learner has entered data into a Text Entry Field, the data can be used throughout the project in many interesting ways. You'll learn how to reference the typed data later. For now, you'll simply learn how to insert and control Text Entry Fields.

Guided Activity 28: Insert a Text Entry Field

1. Open **TextEntryMe** from the Storyline360Data_SecondEdition folder.

2. Open slide **1.2 It's All About You.**

3. Insert a Text Entry Field.

   ❏ select the **Insert** tab on the Ribbon

   ❏ from the **Interactive Objects** group, click **Input**

   ❏ from the bottom of the Inputs, **Data Entry** group, select **Text Entry Field**

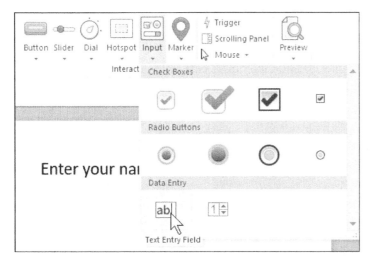

   ❏ draw a Text Entry Field anywhere on the slide

4. Apply a Shape Style to the Text Entry Field.

   ❏ with the **Text Entry Field** selected, click the **Format** tab on the Ribbon

   ❏ from the **Shape Styles** area, select **any style** that you like

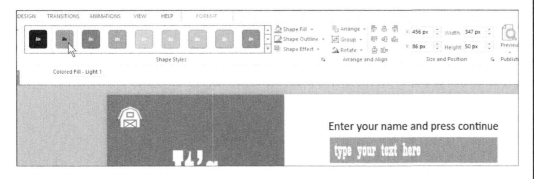

5. Format the text in the Text Entry Field.

   ❏ with the **Text Entry Field** selected, click the **Home** tab on the Ribbon

   ❏ select a **Font**, **Font Size**, **Font Color**, and paragraph alignment that work well with the Shape Style you selected during the previous step

6. Replace the Text Entry Field text and position it on the slide.

   ❏ replace the placeholder text in the Text Entry Field with **type your name here**

   ❏ position the Text Entry Field below the words "Enter your name and press continue"

   ❏ resize the Text Entry Field similar to the image below

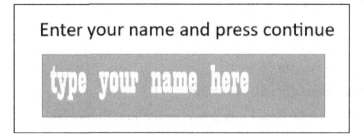

7. Rename the Text Entry Field.

   ❏ at the left of the Timeline, change the name Text Entry to **Learner Name**

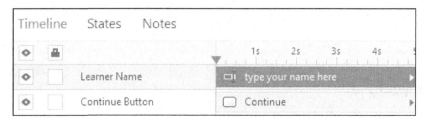

8. Preview the slide.

9. Type your name into the Text Entry Field.

   The text you just typed has been stored within a Variable. During the next activity, you will learn how to use Variables and Triggers that allow you to reference the text.

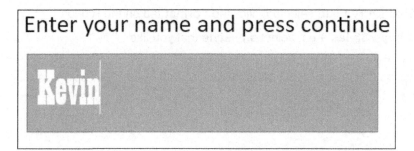

10. Close the preview.

11. Save the project.

Variables

Variables serve as buckets for data. The data can be used to provide feedback to the learner and/or allow you as the developer to create conditional scenarios. For instance, you could use a variable to capture the learner's name. Once the name has been captured by the variable, the name can be displayed throughout the lesson.

Guided Activity 29: Manage a Variable

1. Ensure that the **TextEntryMe** project is still open.

2. Ensure that slide **1.2** is open.

3. Manage the variable.

   ☐ on the **Triggers** window, click **Manage project variables**

The **Variables** dialog box opens. Every time you insert a Text Entry Field in Storyline, a variable is created so it has the capability to store any typed data. The default name, TextEntry, can be changed.

   ☐ click one time on the current variable name (TextEntry) and rename the variable **learnerName**

Note: Variable names cannot contain spaces or special characters such as exclamation marks and question marks. In the image below, the variable is named with a mixed case naming convention known as **camel casing**.

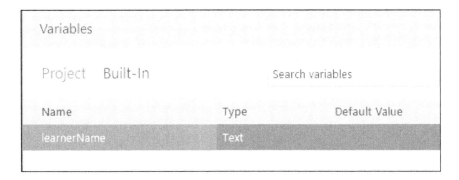

   ☐ click the **OK** button

Guided Activity 30: Reference a Variable

1. Ensure that the **TextEntryMe** project is still open.

2. Open slide **1.3**.

3. Reference a Variable.

   ☐ on the slide, double-click the **Click to add text** sentence

   ☐ on the Ribbon, click the **Insert** tab

   ☐ from the **Text** group, click **Reference**

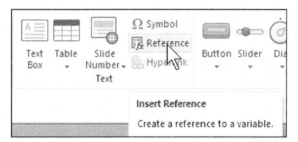

The References dialog box opens. The **learnerName** variable is available, and because it's the only variable in the project, it's also selected.

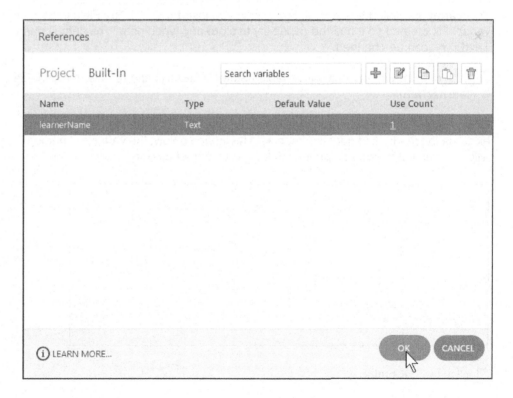

   ☐ click the **OK** button

Storyline inserts a reference to the **learnerName** variable that is distinguishable by the percent signs. In the future, you can insert a reference to a variable by typing it yourself and including the percent signs. Be careful because if you misspell the variable, Storyline has no way to alert you to the error. In case of a spelling error, the data stored by the variable will not appear on the slide.

4. Preview the **scene**.

5. When you get to the **It's All About You** slide, type your name into the Text Entry Field and then click the **Continue** button.

   And like magic, the name is referenced from the learnerName variable and inserted onto the slide.

6. Close the Preview.

7. Save your work.

8. Close the project.

Conditional Triggers

You've learned how to create several triggers during previous activities. You can set up triggers so that they work only **IF** specific conditions are met. On slide 1.2, learners are expected to type their name into the text entry field. However, learners can leave the field empty and still continue with the lesson. You're going to add a condition to the slide's Continue button that requires the learner to type something into the Text Entry Field before being allowed to leave the slide.

Guided Activity 31: Add a Condition to a Button

1. Open **ConditionalTriggerMe** from the Storyline360Data_SecondEdition folder.

2. Open slide **1.2 It's All About You.**

3. Add a Condition to the button Trigger.

   ❑ on the **Triggers** window, select the **Continue Button** Trigger

   ❑ on the top of the **Triggers** window, click **Edit the selected trigger**

   ❑ in the **Condition** area, click **+ if**

   ❑ choose **learnerName**

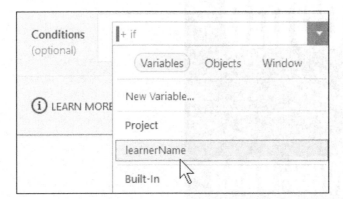

   ❑ click the = **Operator**

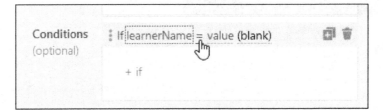

❑ choose **is not equal to**

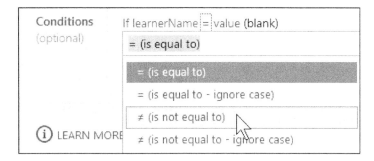

❑ ensure the **Value** field remains **[blank]**

Leaving the Value field [blank] is equivalent to **null**, meaning the learner doesn't type anything into the Text Entry Field.

❑ click the **OK** button

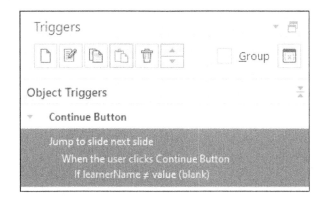

4. Preview the scene.

5. When you get to the **It's All About** you slide, click the **Continue** button without typing anything in the Text Entry Field.

   Thanks to the condition you added to the button's trigger, the lesson does not advance.

6. Type your name into the Text Entry Field and then click the Continue button.

   The lesson moves forward as expected.

7. Close the Preview.

Layers and Conditional Triggers
Confidence Check

1. Still working on slide **1.2 It's All About You,** create a new layer.

2. Name the new layer **Name Required Message**.

3. Using the **Insert** tab on the Ribbon, insert a **Rectangular Caption (No Pointer)** on the **Name Required Message** layer with the following text:

   We really need your name before you can continue!

4. On the **Base Layer**, add a **Conditional Trigger** to the Continue button that will show the **Name Required Message** layer **IF** the learner leaves the Text Entry Field blank.

Trigger Wizard		×
Action	Show layer	
Layer	Name Required Message	
When	When the user clicks	
Object	Continue Button	
Conditions (optional)	If learnerName = value (blank)	
	+ if	

LEARN MORE...   OK   CANCEL

5. Preview the scene.

6. When you get to the **It's All About You** slide, click the **Continue** button without typing anything in the Text Entry Field.

   Thanks to the two conditions you added to the button's trigger, the lesson does not advance *and* the layer containing your "We really need your name before you can continue!" message opens.

7. Type your name into the Text Entry Field and then click the **Continue** button.

   The lesson moves forward as expected.

8. Close the Preview.

9. Save and close the project.

iCONLOGiC

"Skills and Drills" Learning

Module 6: Tables and Number Variables

In This Module You Will Learn About:

- Tables, page 110
- Calculation Variables, page 113

And You Will Learn To:

- Insert a Table, page 110
- Create Variables that Calculate, page 113
- Adjust a Variable with a Trigger, page 117

Tables

Tables are a collection of cells made up into vertical components (columns) and horizontal components (rows). In Storyline, tables are typically used to align and display tabular data.

Guided Activity 32: Insert a Table

1. Open **TableMe** from the Storyline360Data_SecondEdition folder.

2. Insert a table.

   ☐ open slide **3.4 Pricing**

   ☐ delete the placeholder containing the words "Delete this placeholder..."

   ☐ from the **Insert** tab on the **Ribbon**, **Text** group, click the **Table** icon

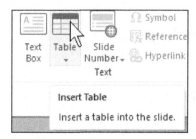

   ☐ hover your mouse over **three** columns and **four** rows (3 x 4) and click once

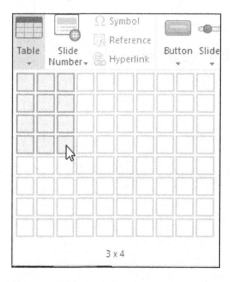

A table containing three columns and four rows is added to the slide.

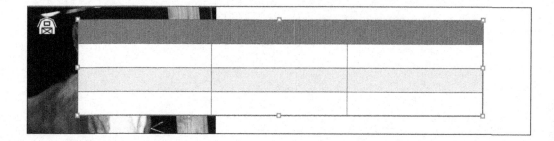

3. Remove the table header.

☐ ensure that the table is selected

☐ from the **Table Tools, Design** tab on the Ribbon, deselect **Header Row**

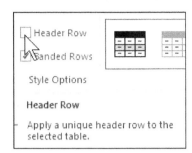

4. Resize and reposition the table.

☐ drag the table onto the slide and position it beneath the Pricing heading

☐ using the resizing handles, resize the table similar to the image shown below

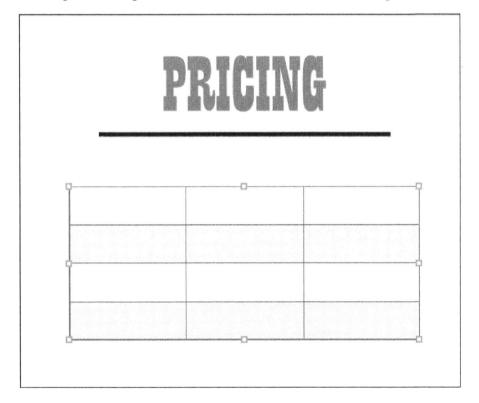

5. Add data to the table.

☐ from the bottom of the Storyline window, click **Notes**

The text you need for the table has already been added to the Notes area. All you'll need to do is copy and paste the text into the appropriate table cells.

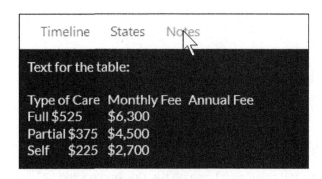

☐ from the Notes area, highlight the phrase **Type of Care**

☐ copy the text to the clipboard

☐ on the slide, right-click in the first table cell and from the Paste Options area, choose **Keep Text Only**

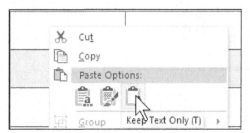

Tables Confidence Check

1. Copy and Paste the remaining table data into the table cells as shown below.

Type of Care	Monthly Fee	Annual Fee
Full	$525	$6,300
Partial	$375	$4,500
Self	$225	$2,700

2. From the **Table Tools** tab on the **Ribbon**, select any **Table Style** that you like.

3. Save and close the project.

Calculation Variables

During the last module, you leveraged variables to allow the learner to see their name throughout the project (page 101). The variable you used during that activity was a text variable. During the next activity, you'll use number variables and triggers to help determine how much hay to feed a horse based on the weight of the horse and number of hay flakes needed. (A hay flake is a portion of a hay bale. Flakes are created as the hay is baled.)

Guided Activity 33: Create Variables that Calculate

1. Open **CalculateMe** from the Storyline360Data_SecondEdition folder.

2. Open slide **5.1**.

3. Insert a Numeric Entry Field.

    ❏ from the **Insert** tab on the Ribbon, **Interactive Objects** group, click **Input**

    ❏ choose **Numeric Entry Field**

    ❏ draw a **Numeric Entry Field** beneath the phrase **Enter the weight of the horse** similar to the image shown below

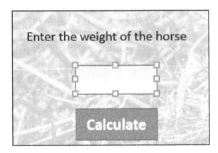

    Adding the Numeric Entry Field automatically creates a variable named NumericEntry. You'll rename the variable next.

4. Rename a variable.

☐ on the **Triggers** window, click **Manage project variables**

The Variables dialog box opens.

☐ click once on the name **NumericEntry** and change it to **HorseWeight**

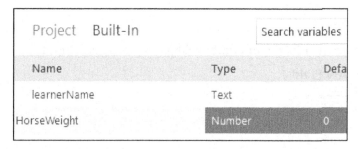

☐ click the **OK** button

5. Create a new Number Variable.

☐ on the **Triggers** window, click **Manage project variables**

☐ from the top right of the dialog box, click **Create a new variable**

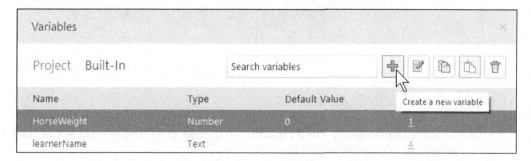

The Variable dialog box reopens. The calculator you are creating will calculate the amount of hay you need based on the weight of the horse. You'll need a number variable to store the weight of the hay.

☐ in the **Name** field, type **PoundsofHay**

☐ from the **Type** drop-down menu, choose **Number**

☐ leave the **Value** set to **0**

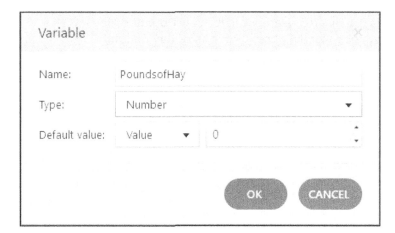

☐ click the **OK** button

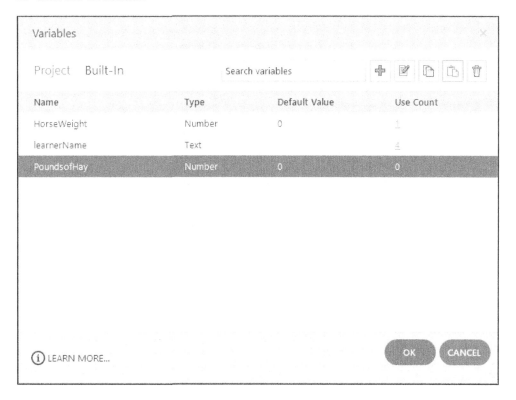

☐ click the **OK** button

NOTES

Variables Confidence Check

1. Still working on slide **5.1**, insert a reference to the new **PoundsofHay** variable into the text box (after the phrase **Pounds of hay needed:**).

   Need help inserting a reference to a variable? See page 102.

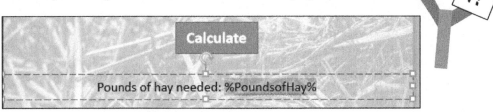

2. Preview the slide.

   Because the variable doesn't yet have anything to calculate, you see the default **0** in the text box.

3. Close the Preview.

4. Save your work.

Guided Activity 34: Adjust a Variable with a Trigger

1. Ensure that the **CalculateMe** project is still open and you're on slide **5.1**.

   You need a trigger that will assign the **PoundsofHay** variable the same value as the **HorseWeight** variable when the user clicks the **Calculate** button on the slide.

2. Create an Adjust variable trigger.

   ☐ on the slide, select the **Calculate** button (on the Timeline, the button has been named **Button 1**)

   ☐ on the **Triggers** window, click **Create a new trigger**

   The Trigger Wizard opens.

   ☐ from the **Action** area choose **Adjust variable**
   ☐ from the **Variable** area, click the link for **learnerName** and choose **PoundsofHay**

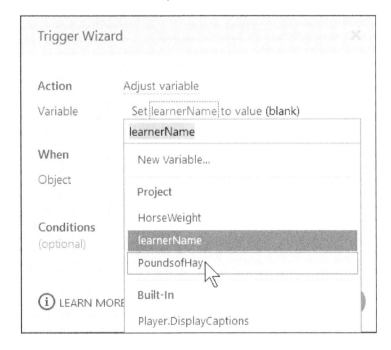

NOTES

☐ click the link for **Value** and choose **Variable**

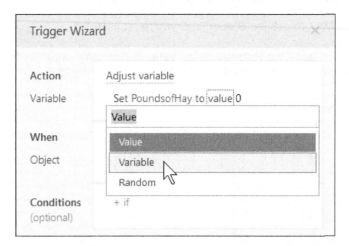

☐ click the link for **Unassigned** and choose **HorseWeight**

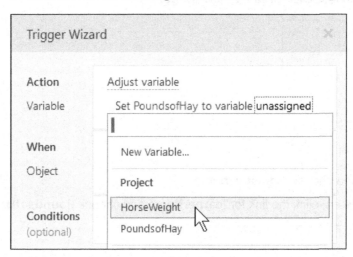

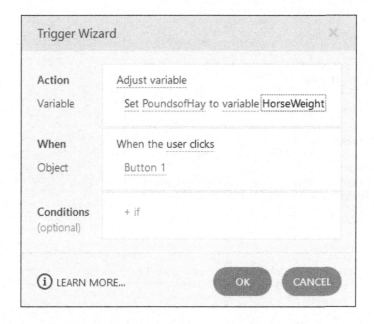

☐ click the **OK** button

To complete the calculation, you need to divide the newly assigned value to the **PoundsofHay** variable and divide it by **100**. You'll do that next.

3. Create a trigger that will divide a value.

☐ on slide **5.1**, select the **Calculate** button (Reminder: On the Timeline, the button is named **Button 1**.)

☐ on the **Triggers** window, click **Create a new trigger**

☐ from the **Action** drop-down menu choose **Adjust variable**

☐ from the list of Variables, choose **PoundsofHay**

☐ from the **Variable** area, click the word **Set**

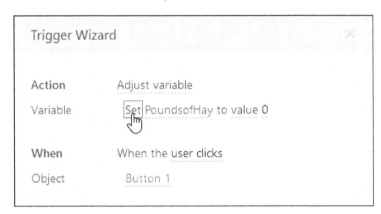

☐ choose / **Divide**

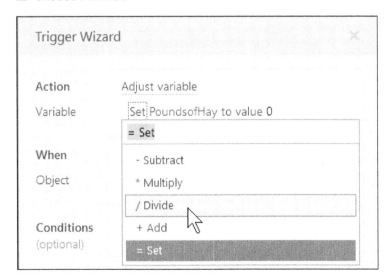

☐ change the value to **100**

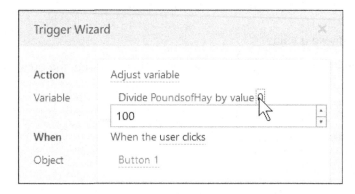

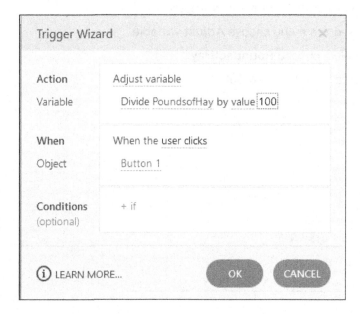

☐ click the **OK** button

4. Preview the slide.

5. Enter a number for the horse weight in pounds, any number is fine, and then click the **Calculate** button.

   The pounds of hay needed for your horse replaces the reference on the slide.

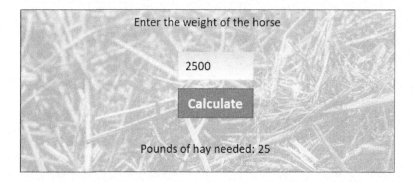

6. Close the preview.

Calculation Variables Confidence Check

1. Still working on slide **5.1**, create a new **Number variable** named **FlakesofHay**.

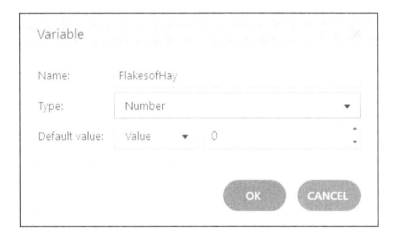

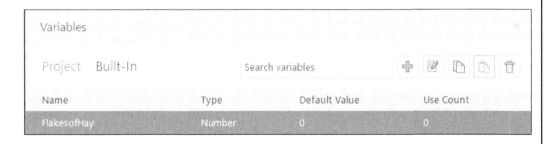

2. On slide **5.1**, insert a reference to the **FlakesofHay** variable after "... the nearest whole flake):"

NOTES

3. Create a new trigger for the **Calculate** button that will assign the **FlakesofHay** variable the same value as the **PoundsofHay** variable when the user clicks the Calculate button.

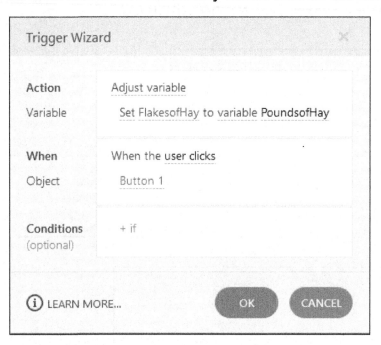

4. Create a new trigger for the **Calculate** button that will divide the newly assigned value to the **FlakesofHay** variable by a Value of **2** (because 2 pounds is the weight of a typical flake of hay).

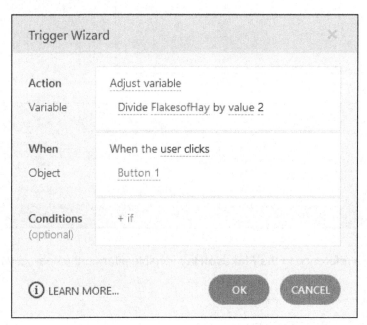

Your Triggers window should look like the image below.

Note: The order of the triggers on the Triggers window is important. Triggers fire from top to bottom. If your triggers are out of order, the calculations won't work correctly. You can reorder triggers on the Triggers window by clicking the **Move the selected trigger up** or **down** arrows next to the Trash icon on the Triggers window.

5. Preview the slide.

6. Enter a number for the horse weight and click the **Calculate** button.

The pounds of hay required for your horse are displayed along with the corresponding number of flakes needed.

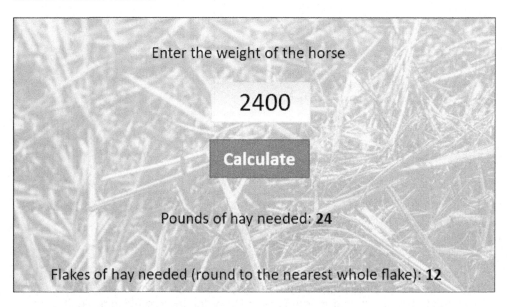

Enter the weight of the horse

2400

Calculate

Pounds of hay needed: **24**

Flakes of hay needed (round to the nearest whole flake): **12**

7. Save and close the project.

iCONLOGiC

"Skills and Drills" Learning

Module 7: Audio, Animation, and Video

In This Module You Will Learn About:

And You Will Learn To:

Adding Audio

While you can import several types of audio files into a Storyline project, the most common audio formats are WAV and MP3.

WAV (WAVE): WAV files are one of the original digital audio standards. Although high in quality, WAV files can be very large. In fact, typical WAV audio files can easily take up to several megabytes of storage per minute of playing time. If your learner has a slow Internet connection, the download time for large files is unacceptable.

MP3 (MPEG Audio Layer III): Developed in Germany by the Fraunhofer Institute, MP3 files are compressed digital audio files. File sizes in this format are typically 90 percent smaller than WAV files.

Text to Speech: Storyline 360 also allows you to convert text to speech out of the box. This feature is particularly useful when you create prototypes or when you do not have the budget to hire voiceover talent.

> **Note:** To learn more about digital audio formats, visit **www.webopedia.com/ DidYouKnow/Computer_Science/2005/digital_audio_formats.asp**.

Guided Activity 35: Insert Audio

1. Open **AudioMe** from the Storyline360Data_SecondEdition folder.

2. Open slide **1.1**.

3. Insert audio onto the slide.

   ☐ select the **Insert** tab on the Ribbon

   ☐ from the **Media** group, click the **Audio** drop-down menu and choose **Audio from File**

The Insert Audio dialog box opens.

   ☐ open the **Storyline360Data_SecondEdition** folder

   ☐ from the **audio** folder, open **s1.1.wav**

The audio is inserted onto the slide. You can tell that audio has been inserted via the speaker icon to the left of the slide and the audio object on the Timeline.

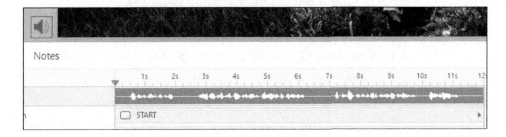

Guided Activity 36: Use Text-to-Speech to Create Audio

1. Ensure that the **AudioMe** project is still open.

2. Open slide **1.2 It's All About You**.

3. Select the **Notes** window.

   Notice that there is a voiceover script for the slide.

4. Use Notes text as Text to Speech audio.

   ☐ select the **Insert** tab on the Ribbon

   ☐ from the **Media** group, click the **Audio** drop-down menu and choose **Text-to-Speech**

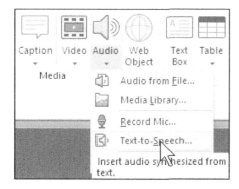

   The Text-to-Speech window opens.

   ☐ click the **Copy From Slide Notes** button

   The text you reviewed on the Notes window is added to the Insert Text-to-Speech dialog box.

---

5. Preview a voice and insert Text to Speech audio.

☐ from the drop-down menu at the **left**, choose **English (US)**

☐ from the next drop-down menu, choose any voice you wish

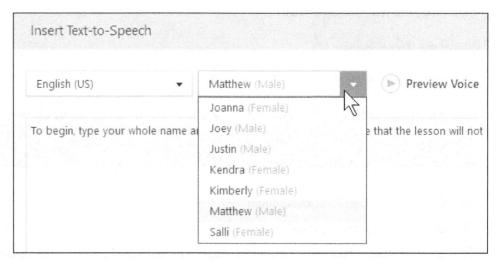

☐ click the **icon** to the left of **Preview Voice**

☐ once you've settled on a voice that you like, click the **Insert** button

Clicking the Insert button instantly creates an audio file. The finished media appears as an audio icon at the left of the slide (shown in the image below).

6. Preview the finished Text-to-Speech audio.

☐ to the left of the slide, right-click the **audio icon** and choose **Preview Audio**

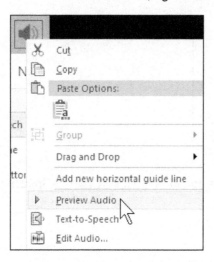

The Text-to-Speech audio sounds fine but the script includes the words "type your *whole* name" when it should only have been "type your name." You could edit the text in the Notes window and reinsert the Text-to-Speech audio. However, you can also edit the audio file and remove the unwanted word, which you'll do next.

Guided Activity 37: Edit Audio

1. Ensure that the **AudioMe** project is still open.

2. Ensure that you're still on slide **1.2**.

3. Open an audio file for editing.

   ❏ on the **Timeline**, double-click the audio waveform (Text-to-Speech 1)

   The Audio Editor opens.

   ❏ at the lower left of the Audio Editor, click the green play icon to move the Playhead along the waveform (the Playhead is the blue vertical line)

   ❏ click the **Pause** button when you hear the narrator say "whole name"

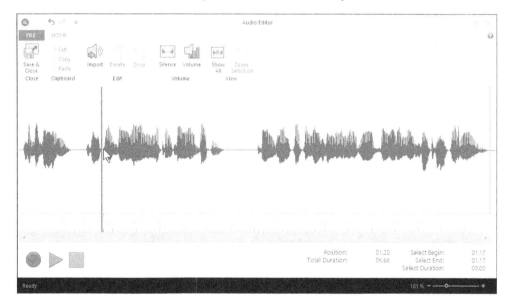

NOTES

4. Zoom closer to the audio file.

   ☐ from the bottom right of the Audio Editor, click the **Zoom** plus sign to zoom significantly closer to the audio file

   Note: The closer you get to the audio file, the easier it will be to select and remove a small portion of the audio.

   ☐ highlight the portion of the audio file that contains the word "whole"

   ☐ click the **Play** button to ensure you have selected only the single word

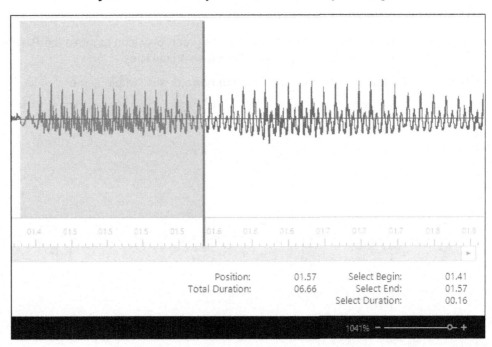

5. Delete a portion of an audio file.

   ☐ with the portion of the audio file containing the word "whole" selected, click the **Delete** icon

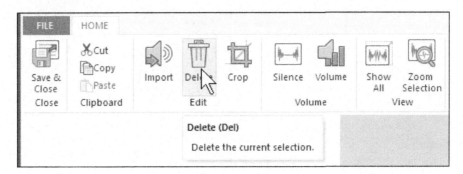

   ☐ click the **Save & Close** button

6. Preview the audio to confirm that the word "whole" has been removed.

   As mentioned earlier, one popular use for Text-to-Speech is to serve as a placeholder for "real" audio. During the next activity, you'll replace the current Text-to-Speech audio with finished audio that has just arrived from your voiceover talent.

Guided Activity 38: Replace Audio

1. Ensure that the **AudioMe** project is still open.

2. Open slide **1.2**.

3. Replace audio.

   ☐ on the **Timeline**, right-click the audio file and choose **Replace Audio > Audio from File**

   ☐ from **Storyline360Data_SecondEdition > audio**, open **s1.2**

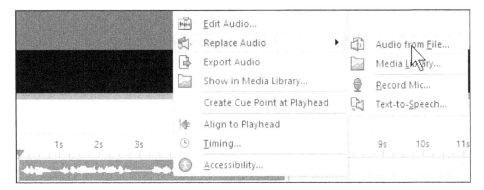

The original audio has been replaced with the "real audio."

4. Preview the new audio.

Inserting Audio Confidence Check

1. Insert the remaining voiceover audio files in the **Storyline360Data_SecondEdition > audio** folder onto the appropriate slides. (The audio files are named so that they match their corresponding scene and slide).

   Note: Not every slide has audio. Also, slide 4.2 has multiple layers. Insert the appropriate audio onto each corresponding slide layer. For instance, audio file **s4.2** needs to be imported onto the slide; **s4.2_Western** needs to be imported onto the **Western** layer.

2. Preview the project to hear the audio.

3. Close the Preview.

4. Save the project.

Recording Audio

As you have already learned, you can easily import audio files into Storyline. However, you can also record your own audio. To record audio, you will need a microphone connected to your computer. Once you've got the microphone, consider the following:

Setup: If you plan to use high-end audio hardware, such as a mixer or preamplifier, plug your microphone into the hardware and then plug the hardware into your computer's "line in" port. Set the volume on your mixer or preamplifier to just under zero as this will minimize distortion.

Microphone placement: The microphone should be positioned four to six inches from your mouth to reduce the chance that nearby sounds are recorded. Ideally, you should position the microphone above your nose and pointed down at your mouth. Also, if you position the microphone just to the side of your mouth, you can soften the sound of the letters **S** and **P**.

Microphone technique: It's a good idea to keep a glass of water close by and, just before recording, take a drink. To eliminate the annoying breathing and lip smack sounds, turn away from the microphone, take a deep breath, exhale, take another deep breath, open your mouth, turn back toward the microphone, and start speaking. Speak slowly. When recording for the first time, many people race through the content. Take your time.

Guided Activity 39: Record Voiceover Audio

1. Ensure that the **AudioMe** project is still open.

2. Open slide **6.1**.

3. Review the existing voiceover script for the slide.

   ❑ at the bottom of the Storyline window, click **Notes**

   The script for the audio you are about to record has already be placed in the Notes panel.

Timeline	States	Notes

   Now let's see how much you can remember about horse care by taking the following quiz.

4. Rehearse recording the voiceover audio.

   ❑ with the **Notes** window open, say the following out loud:

   Now let's see how much you can remember about horse care by taking the following quiz.

   Note: As you rehearse the voiceover script, consider how fast you're speaking. When rehearsing and/or recording voiceover audio, the tendency for many people is to talk too fast. The goal is to record the audio at a medium-paced, comfortable speed.

5. Set the audio recording options.

    ❏ click the **Insert** tab on the Ribbon

    ❏ from the **Media** group, choose **Audio > Options**

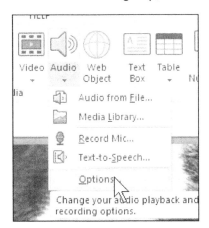

The Audio Options dialog box opens. You can use this dialog box to select a specific microphone for use during the recording process. This is especially helpful if you have more than one microphone attached to your computer. You can also increase or decrease the microphone's volume levels.

    ❏ from the **Audio Recording** area, select your microphone as necessary (in most cases, the microphone selected by default will work fine)

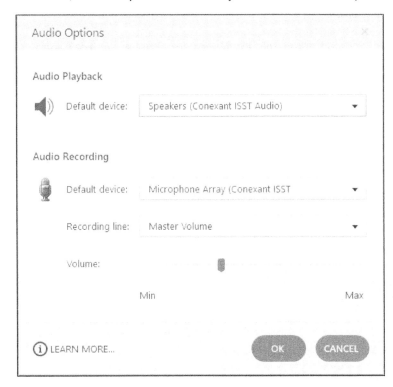

    ❏ click the **OK** button

6. Open the Record Microphone dialog box.

   ☐ click the **Insert** tab on the Ribbon

   ☐ from the **Media** group, choose **Audio > Record Mic**

The Record Microphone dialog box opens.

7. Display the Narration Script.

   ☐ at the right side of the dialog box, click **Narration Script**

The text you typed, and rehearsed, into the **Notes** area appears in a separate window, the Narration Script window. Having the text so close at hand is helpful during the recording process.

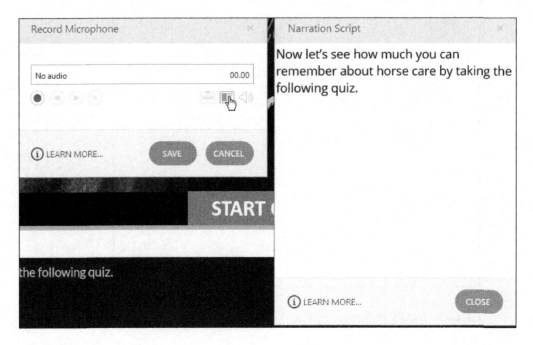

8. Record voiceover audio.

❏ at the far left of the Record Microphone dialog box, click **Record**

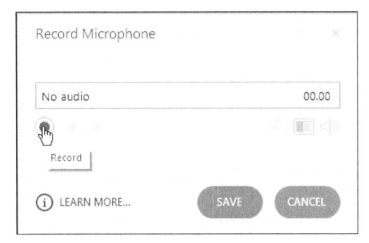

❏ using the Narration Script window, record the following: **Now let's see how much you can remember about horse care by taking the following quiz.**

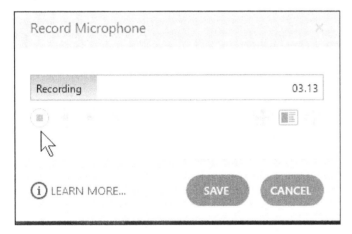

❏ click the **Stop** button
❏ click the **Save** button

9. On the Timeline, notice that an audio object has been added, this is the voiceover you just recorded.

10. Preview the slide to hear the new audio.

11. Close the Preview.

12. Close the slide.

13. Save and close the project.

NOTES

Adding Animation

You can control the way an object enters a slide via Entrance Animations and control the way an object leaves a slide via Exit Animations. Once you've applied an animation to an object, you can control the timing of the animation and choose from several effects, such as Fades, Swivel, Wheel, and Random bars.

Guided Activity 40: Animate an Object

1. Open the **Animate_VideoMe** project from the Storyline360Data_SecondEdition folder.

2. Open slide **1.2 It's All About You**.

3. Animate an object.

   ☐ on the Timeline, select the **Learner Name** object

   On the slide, the **Learner Name** object is the text entry field containing the words "type your name here."

   ☐ from the **Animations** tab on the Ribbon, **Entrance Animations**, click the **Animate** icon

   ☐ choose **Fly In**

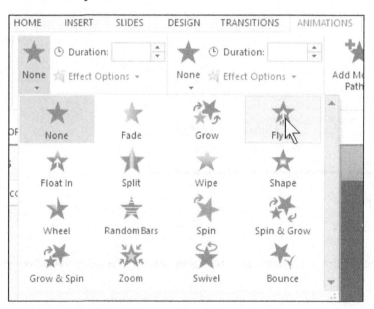

The text entry field gets an animation icon, a **star** located in the upper left of the object.

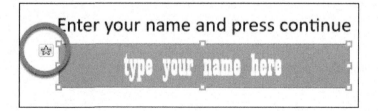

4. Preview the slide and notice that the text entry field enters the slide from the bottom.

5. Close the Preview.

6. Modify the animation.

 ☐ on the slide, select the text entry field

 ☐ from the left of the **Animations** tab on the Ribbon, click the **Effect Options** drop-down menu and choose **From Right**

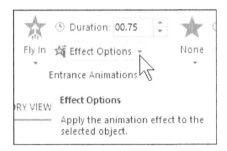

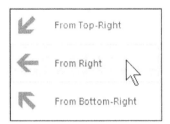

7. Preview the slide again.

 This time the text entry field enters the slide from the right side of the screen.

8. Close the Preview.

Guided Activity 41: Animate Text

1. Ensure that the **Animate_VideoMe** project is still open.

2. Open slide **3.2**.

3. Animate the bulleted list.

   ☐ on the slide, select the text box containing the bulleted list

   ☐ from the **Animations** tab on the Ribbon, **Entrance Animations**, click the **Animate** icon and choose **Fade**

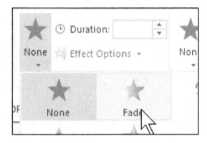

4. Preview the slide.

   Notice that the entire text box fades in. Next you'll modify the animation so that the text fades in one paragraph at a time.

5. Close the Preview.

6. Animate text by Sequence.

   ☐ on the slide, ensure that the text box containing the bulleted list is still selected

   ☐ within the **Animations** tab on the Ribbon, **Entrance Animations** group, click **Effect Options**

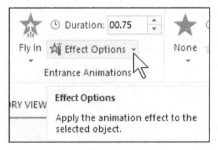

   ☐ from the **Sequence** area, choose **By Paragraph**

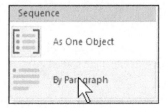

7. On the Timeline, notice that there is a triangle to the left of the text box you animated.

8. Click the triangle to expand the animations and notice that each paragraph in the text box is represented on the Timeline.

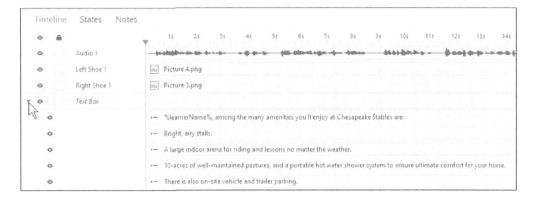

9. Use the Timeline to stagger the appearance of the text.

   ☐ on the Timeline, drag the **Bright, airy stalls** to the **right** by approximately one or two seconds

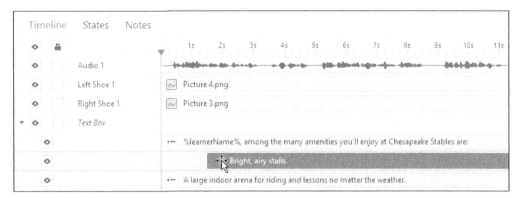

Timing Animations Confidence Check

1. Still on slide **3.2**, drag each of the paragraph objects on the Timeline to the **right** so they are staggered by approximately **3 seconds**.

2. Preview the slide.

   Notice that the text fades in and is somewhat synchronized with the voiceover audio.

3. Close the Preview.

4. If necessary, adjust the paragraphs on the Timeline so that the text is synchronized with the voiceover audio as closely as possible.

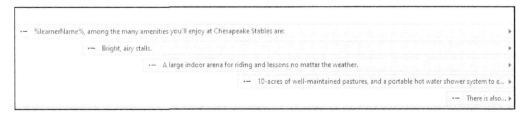

5. Save the project.

NOTES

Guided Activity 42: Animate an Image

1. Ensure that the **Animate_VideoMe** project is still open.

2. Open slide **6.1**.

3. Preview the slide and notice that there is a horse trotting in place. The trotting is not a Storyline animation. Instead, the image is an animated GIF that was created in Adobe Photoshop and then imported onto the slide. You learned how to import pictures on page 49.

4. Close the Preview.

5. Add an entrance animation to an image.

   ❏ on slide **6.1**, select the animated horse image

   ❏ within the **Animations** tab on the Ribbon, **Entrance Animations** group, click **Animate** and choose **Fly In**

6. Preview the slide and notice that the animated horse flies onto the slide from the bottom.

7. Close the Preview.

8. Change the animation options.

   ❏ on the slide, ensure that the animated image of the horse is still selected

   ❏ from the **Animations** tab on the Ribbon, click the **Effect Options** drop-down menu and choose **From Left**

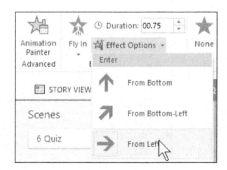

9. Preview the slide again and notice that the animated horse flies onto the slide from the left. The speed is a bit too fast. You'll slow it down next.

10. Close the Preview.

11. Change the animation speed.

    ❏ on the slide, ensure that the animated GIF image of the horse is still selected

    ❏ from the **Animations** tab on the Ribbon, **Entrance Animations** group, change the **Duration** to **3.00**

12. Preview the slide to see the new animation duration.

13. Close the Preview.

Guided Activity 43: Create an Animation Completes Trigger

1. Ensure that the **Animate_VideoMe** project is still open.

2. Still working on slide **6.1**, select the **horse animation**.

3. On the **Timeline**, notice that we named the horse object **animated horse**.

4. On the **States** window, notice that there is a **Facing front** State that we have already created for you. (You learned how to work with States beginning on page 84.)

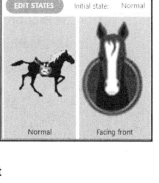

5. Create a trigger that changes the state of an object when an animation completes.

    ☐ on the **Triggers** window, create a new trigger

    ☐ from the **Action** area, click the link and choose **Change state of**

    ☐ click the **Object** link and choose **animated horse**

    ☐ from the **State** area, click the link and choose **Facing front**

    ☐ from the **When** area, click the link and choose **Animation completes**

    ☐ ensure the **Object** is **animated horse** and the **Animation** is **Entrance**

    ☐ click the **OK** button

6. Preview the slide to see the appearance of the horse image change to Facing front once the animation completes.

7. When finished, close the preview.

Motion Paths

Although it's easy to add animations to an object that allow for simple movement, Motion Paths allow you to move slide objects from one location to another along a path and to control exactly where the animation starts and stops. Unlike simple animations, you can apply multiple Motion Paths to an object. In addition, Motion Paths can be associated with triggers to initiate an object's motion along a path.

Guided Activity 44: Create a Simple Motion Path

1. Ensure that the **Animate_VideoMe** project is still open.

2. Add a motion path to an image.

❑ still working on slide **6.1**, select the horse animation

❑ on the **Ribbon**, select the **Animations** tab

❑ from the **Motion Paths** group, click **Add Motion Path**

❑ from the **Basic** section, select **Lines**

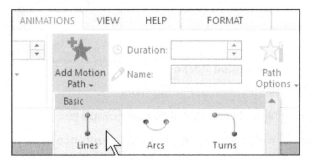

On the slide, notice that a few things have changed about the horse image. There is a blue line starting in the middle of the image—this is the Motion Path. Second, the Motion Path has a green dot indicating the default origin of the Motion Path. Lower down (beneath the Start Quiz button), there is a faded version of the image with a red dot that indicates where the image will end up after the motion path has completed.

3. Preview the slide.

   The horse drops down and passes through the Start Quiz button. But, what happened to the first animation where the horse moved across the screen? The Motion Path is superseding the other animation. You'll fix that next.

4. Close the Preview.

5. Control when the Motion Path occurs.

   ☐ with the **horse motion path** selected, select the **Move animated horse along Line Motion Path 1** trigger on the **Triggers** window

   ☐ click the **Edit the selected trigger** icon

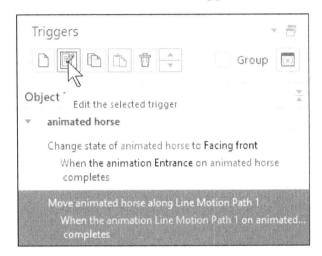

   ☐ from the **When** area, click the link and choose **animation completes**

   ☐ in the **Animation** area, click the link and choose **Entrance**

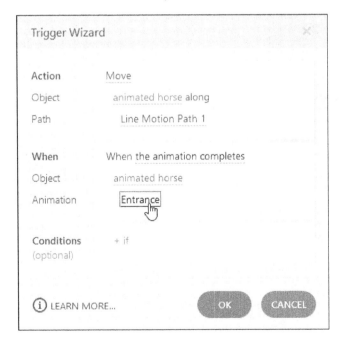

   ☐ click the **OK** button

6. Preview the slide.

   The entrance animation supersedes the Motion Path animation. Next you'll change the ending point for the Motion Path so that the horse image does not go below the slide.

7. Close the Preview.

8. Edit the Motion Path's End Point.

   ❏ with the horse animation selected, locate the red circle beneath the image of the horse below the slide

   ❏ drag the red dot up until it is just above the Start Quiz button

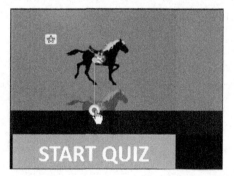

9. Preview the slide and notice that the Motion Path ends just above the button.

10. Close the Preview.

11. Save your work.

Adding Video

You can insert video files using just about any video format into Storyline projects and from video sharing services, such as YouTube and Vimeo. There are also videos available for import in the Media Library.

Guided Activity 45: Insert a Video onto a Slide

1. Ensure that the **Animate_VideoMe** project is still open.

2. Open slide **7.1**.

3. Insert a video onto the slide.

   ❏ from the **Insert** tab on the Ribbon, **Media** group, click the **Video** drop-down menu and choose **Video from file**

   ❏ from the **Storyline360Data_SecondEdition** folder, open the **images_videos** folder

   ❏ open **SidesaddleClinic.wmv**

   The SidesaddleClinic video is inserted onto the slide.

4. Preview the slide to see the video.

   Note: The video was created using a program called VideoScribe. You can learn more about the tool at https://www.videoscribe.co.

5. Close the Preview.

6. Save your work.

Guided Activity 46: Embed an External Video

1. Ensure that the **Animate_VideoMe** project is still open.

2. Open slide **7.2**.

3. Open the Notes window.

   We already found a video on YouTube about the different types of hay. We've copied the code needed for learners to view the video directly from YouTube and pasted the code into the Notes panel for you. You will use the code as you embed the video in Storyline.

4. Highlight and copy the video code in the Notes window to the clipboard.

5. Embed a video onto the slide.

   ☐ from the **Insert** tab on the Ribbon, **Media** group, click the **Video** drop-down menu and choose **Video from website**

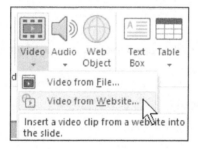

   The Insert Video from Website dialog box opens.

   ☐ **paste** the code you copied to the clipboard into the text field

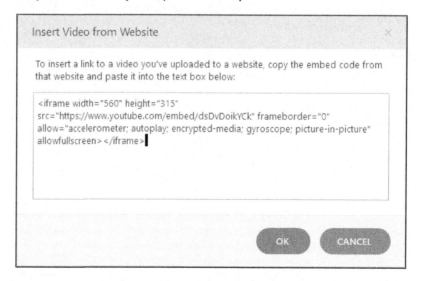

   ☐ click the **OK** button

A gray box appears in the middle of the screen.

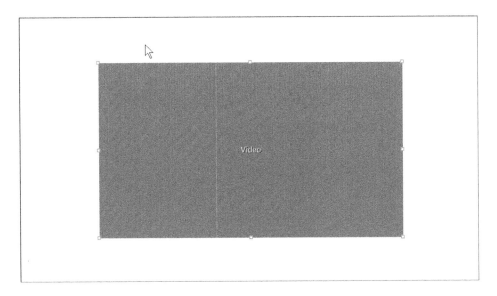

6. Preview the slide.

   Unlike side-saddle video you inserted earlier, web videos do not appear when you preview. To see the web video, you need to Publish the slide.

7. Close the Preview.

8. Publish a single slide.

   ☐ choose **File > Publish**

   The Publish dialog box opens.

   ☐ from the list of categories at the left, click **Web**
   ☐ from the **Publish** area, click the **Entire Project** link and choose **A single slide**
   ☐ from the slide drop-down menu, choose **7.2 Types of Hay**

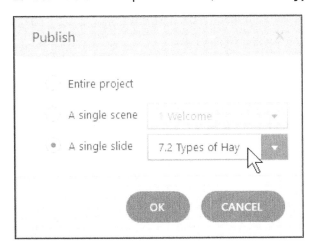

   ☐ click the **OK** button
   ☐ click the **Publish** button

NOTES

The Publish Successful dialog box opens.

☐ click the **View Project** button

The published slide opens in your web browser, and you can play the embedded YouTube video.

9. Close the browser and return to Storyline.

10. Close the Publish Successful dialog box.

Embedding Videos Confidence Check

1. Still working in the **Animate_VideoMe** project, open slide **3.3**.

2. On the slide, select the icon for the **hay**.

3. Create a new Trigger with a **Lightbox slide** action that goes to slide **7.2**.

Lightbox slides are pretty cool. When viewed by the learner they appear on top of the current slide. You'll see the effect next when you preview the project.

4. Preview the entire project.

5. Use the menu at the left to jump to **Levels of Horse Care**.

6. Click the hay icon.

   The Lightbox slide appears on top of the current slide.

7. Close the Preview and return to Storyline.

8. Insert a new blank slide into Scene **7**.

9. Minimize Storyline and, using your web browser, go to **YouTube.com**.

10. Find any video on YouTube about horse care.

   Note: You need YouTube's Embed code for use in Storyline. The steps for finding YouTube's Embed Code are shown below but can vary from browser to browser. The steps that follow are the most common steps.

11. From beneath the video, click **Share**.

The Share dialog box opens.

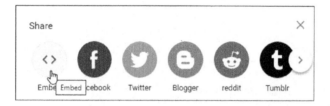

12. Click **Embed**.

   The Embed Video window opens.

13. Select and copy the code in the Embed Video window to the clipboard.

14. Return to Storyline, insert a **Video from website** onto your new slide and then paste the code into the text field.

15. Publish just the new slide and view it in your web browser to see the embedded video.

16. When finished, close the browser.

17. Back in Storyline, save and close the project.

iCONLOGiC

"Skills and Drills" Learning

Module 8: Quizzes

In This Module You Will Learn About:

- Quizzing, page 152

And You Will Learn To:

- Insert a Multiple Choice Slide, page 152

- Insert a Matching Drop-down Slide, page 156

- Insert a Freeform Drag and Drop Quiz Slide, page 158

- Insert a Quiz Result Slide, page 161

Quizzing

Learning can be exhausting. If you think about it, there's only so much learning that can effectively occur over a set amount of time. If you are a trainer, you can elect to force feed information to your students. However, without regularly scheduled breaks, the ability of your students to both learn and retain information is minimized. Beyond giving breaks, you may encourage your learners to openly discuss what they are learning during class. Discussing lessons taught in class greatly improves the students' experience, enhances their understanding of the concepts, and increases their retention of the material.

An eLearning session has no live trainer and no classmates. How is a learner supposed to share the knowledge gained during class when the learner is alone? One solution is to add a quiz. In addition to providing you, as the instructional designer, a way to measure the effectiveness of the course content, the students will be able to think about what they have learned as they answer quiz questions.

Storyline includes a wonderful array of Quiz Slides, including Multiple Choice, True/False, Matching, Fill-in-the-blank, Pick One or Many, and even Drag-and-Drop. During the activities that follow, you'll get a chance to add a quiz and a few questions to the Chesapeake Stables project.

Guided Activity 47: Insert a Multiple Choice Slide

1. Open the **QuizMe** project from the Storyline360Data_SecondEdition folder.

2. Open slide **6.1**.

3. Insert a Multiple Choice Quiz Slide.

   ☐ from the **Slides** tab on the Ribbon, **Quizzing** group, click **Graded Question**

   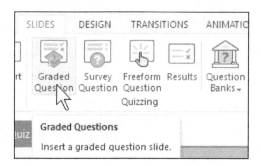

   The Insert Slide dialog box opens.

   ☐ at the top of the dialog box, select **Multiple Choice**

   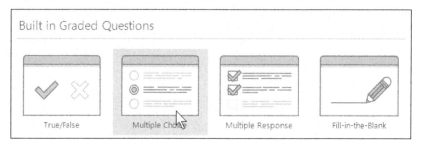

   ☐ click the **Insert Slide** button

The question opens in **Form View**. You can use this view to add the question text and set up question options, such as feedback text and point values.

4. Add a question.

    ☐ in the **Enter the question** area, type **How many pounds of hay should you feed your horse a day if your horse weighs 1,000 pounds?**

5. Add the Choices.

    ☐ to the right of answer **A**, click in the **Choice** area and type **2**

    ☐ to the right of answer **B**, click in the **Choice** area and type **10**

    ☐ to the right of answer **C**, click in the **Choice** area and type **5**

    ☐ to the right of answer **D**, click in the **Choice** area and type **20**

6. Set the correct answer.

    ☐ to the left of answer **B (10)**, click the radio button

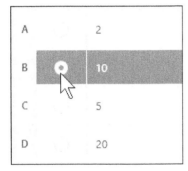

7. Change the point value of the question to 25.

    ☐ at the bottom of the Form View, notice the **Feedback** area

    ☐ to the right of the **Correct** Feedback option, click the number **10** in the **Points** area and replace the number with **25**

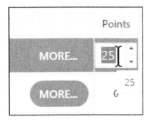

NOTES

8. Edit the Feedback text.

    ☐ to the left of the **25**, click the **More** button

    The resulting **Feedback** dialog box presents you with an opportunity to change the Feedback text, add audio, and control where the learner goes after answering the question correctly (Branch to the following).

    ☐ at the top of the Feedback dialog box, replace the existing text with **That's right! You feed 2 pounds of hay per 100 pounds of horse.**

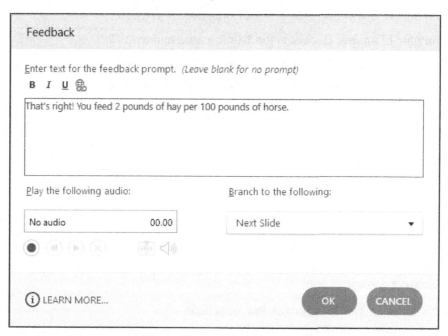

    ☐ click the **OK** button

    On the Ribbon, notice that the options are now question-slide specific. For instance, you can add **Audio** to the slide, insert **Media**, change the number of **Attempts**, and more.

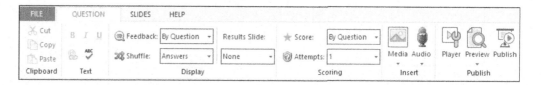

9. Switch to Slide View.

    ☐ from the **Question** window (at the far right of the Storyline window), click **Slide View**

You can use the Question window to quickly switch between Slide and Form View, allowing you to edit the question options and text as needed. Notice also that two additional layers have been added in Slide Layers. These new layers contain the feedback text. You can edit the content on the layers as you can with any Storyline layer.

Your question slide should look like this:

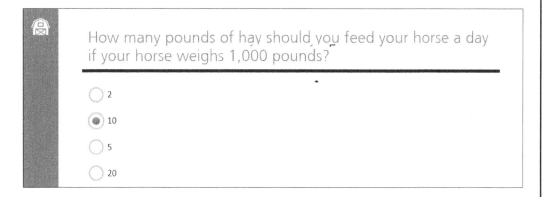

10. Preview the slide and answer the question.

    If you answer the question correctly and click Submit (the checkmark in the lower right of the slide is the Submit button), you'll see the feedback text you edited a moment ago. If you answer incorrectly and click Submit, you'll see the default feedback text.

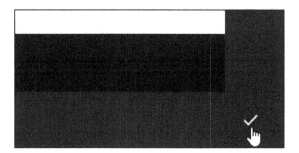

11. Close the Preview.

12. Save your work.

Guided Activity 48: Insert a Matching Drop-down Slide

1. Ensure that the QuizMe project is still open.

2. Insert another quiz slide.

    ☐ on the **Scenes** window, select slide **6.2**

    ☐ from the **Slides** tab on the Ribbon, **Quizzing** group, click **Graded Question**

    The Insert Slide dialog box reopens.

    ☐ select **Matching Drop-down**

    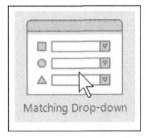

    ☐ click the **Insert Slide** button

    The question opens in Form View.

3. Add the question.

    ☐ in the **Enter the question** area, type **Match each monthly price with the appropriate level of care.**

4. Add the Choices and Matches.

    ☐ for **Choice A**, type **Full** into the **Choice** column

    ☐ to the right of **Full**, type **$525** into the **Match** column

5. Edit the remaining options to match the picture below.

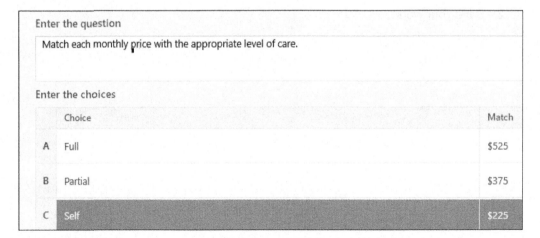

6. Switch to Slide View.

7. Preview the slide.

8. From the drop-down menu, choose the appropriate price for each level of care and then click the Submit button to see how well you did.

9. Close the Preview.

Quiz Confidence Check

1. Insert a **True/False** slide beneath slide **6.3** that matches the picture below.

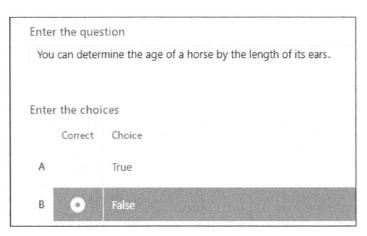

2. Use **Form View** to change the points for the correct answer on slides **6.3** and **6.4** to **25**.

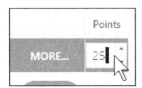

3. Save the project.

Guided Activity 49: Insert a Freeform Drag and Drop Quiz Slide

1. Ensure that the QuizMe project is still open.

2. Insert a Freeform quiz slide.

   ☐ select slide **6.4**

   ☐ from the **Slides** tab on the Ribbon, **Quizzing** group, click **Freeform Question**

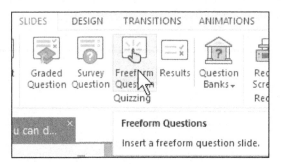

   The Insert Slide dialog box reopens.

   ☐ select **Drag and Drop**

   ☐ click the **Insert Slide** button

   Unlike the other questions you inserted, after inserting the Drag and Drop slide, you are taken to Slide View instead of Form View. You'll be inserting four images onto the question slide, something you cannot do while in the Form View.

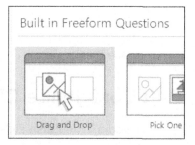

3. Apply a layout.

   ☐ right-click the slide background and choose **Apply Layout > Question**

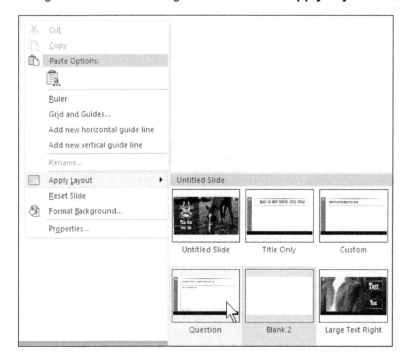

---

4. Add instructions to the slide.

   ❏ click in the title placeholder and type **Drag the riding style images to their correct target**

5. Insert four images onto the slide.

   ❏ click the **Insert** tab on the **Ribbon**

   ❏ from the **Media** group, click **Picture** and choose **Picture from File**

   ❏ from the **Storyline360Data_SecondEdition** folder, open **images_videos**

   ❏ select and **open** the following **four** images: **english, english-target, western**, and **western-target**

6. Move the images around the slide until your slide is similar to the picture below.

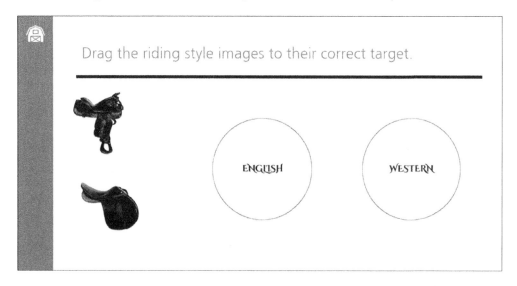

7. Associate the images (the Drag Items) with the circles (the Drop Targets).

   ❏ switch to **Form View**

   ❏ from the **Drag Items and drop targets** area, row **A**, **Drag Item** drop-down menu, choose **western.png**

   ❏ from the row **A**, **Drop Target** drop-down menu, choose **western-target.png**

   ❏ from the row **B**, **Drag Item** drop-down menu, choose **english.png**

   ❏ from the row **B**, **Drop Target** drop-down menu, choose **english-target.png**

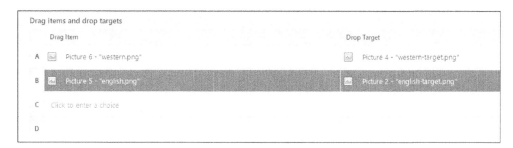

8. From the **Set feedback and branching** area, change the **Points** to **25**.

9. Change the number of Attempts for a correct answer.

 ☐ from the **Question** tab on the Ribbon, **Scoring** group, change the Attempts to **2**

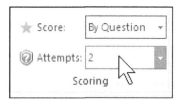

10. Preview the slide.

Drag either saddle to either drop target. Then click the Submit button to check your answer (the check mark in the lower right of the Preview). If you get the answer wrong, you have a second attempt (thanks to the two attempts that you just set up for the slide).

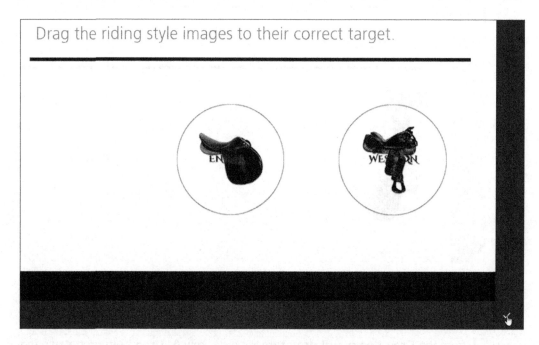

11. Close the preview.

12. Save your work.

Guided Activity 50: Insert a Quiz Result Slide

1. Ensure that the QuizMe project is still open.

2. Select slide **6.5**.

3. Insert a Quiz Results Slide.

   ☐ click **Slides** on the Ribbon and, from the **Quizzing** group, click **Results**

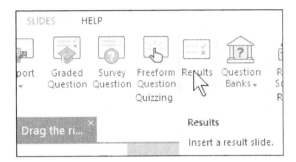

The Insert Slide dialog box reopens.

   ☐ at the top of the dialog box, select **Graded Result Slide**

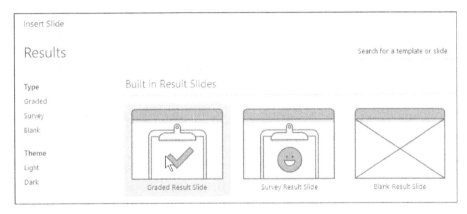

   ☐ click the **Insert Slide** button

The Result Slide Properties dialog box opens. By default, all of the questions you have added to the quiz will be counted in the final score.

   ☐ at the bottom of the dialog box, change the **Passing Score** to **75**

   ☐ click the **OK** button

---

4. Allow users to print the quiz results.

   ☐ from the **Result Tools** tab on the Ribbon, click **Design**

   ☐ from the **Insert** group, click **Print Button**

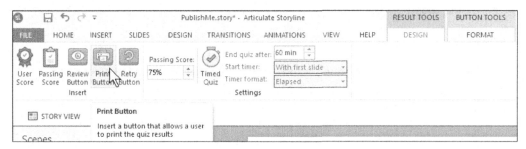

5. On the slide, draw a button similar to the image below.

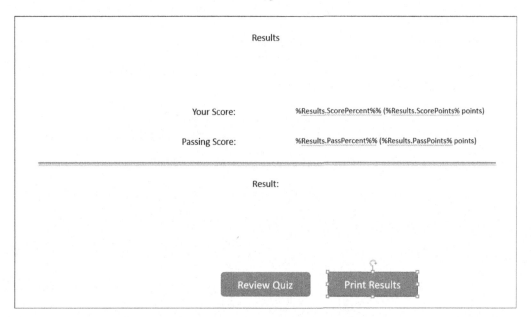

Quiz Results Confidence Check

1. Ensure that all of the questions in the quiz are worth 25 points.

2. Preview the **scene** and take the quiz. (When finished with the quiz this time, you'll see the results slide.)

3. Close the Preview.

4. Add a **Retry Button** to the Quiz Results slide. (Hint: You'll find this option in the same location as the Print Button you learned about a moment ago.)

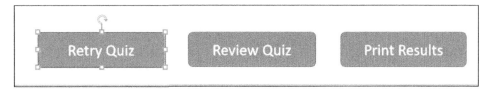

5. Preview the scene again and test the Retry Quiz button.

6. Close the Preview

7. Save your work and close the project.

Notes

iCONLOGiC
"Skills and Drills" Learning

Module 9: Publishing

In This Module You Will Learn About:

And You Will Learn To:

Player Settings

You will soon be publishing your eLearning project. Prior to publishing, you can customize the **Player**, the window within which your lesson will be displayed. When customizing the Player, you can add branding (including your logo, corporate colors, and language), and you can elect to include a Menu, Glossary, and even a Resources area.

Guided Activity 51: Edit Player Properties

1. Open the **PublishMe** project from the Storyline360Data_SecondEdition folder.

2. Open the Player Properties dialog box.

    ❑ select the **Home** tab on the Ribbon

    ❑ from the **Publish** group, click **Player**

3. Edit the Player tabs.

    ❑ from the top left of the dialog box, click **Features**

    ❑ from the **Player Tabs** area, deselect **Resources**

    The word "Resources" at the top right hand side of the Preview window is removed.

    ❑ from the **Sidebar** area, ensure that **Menu** is selected

    ❑ ensure that **Notes** is deselected

    ❑ ensure that **Glossary** is deselected

4. Add a Title.

    ❏ from the **Features** area, ensure **Title** is selected

    ❏ change the **Title** to **Chesapeake Stables**

    ❏ from the **Sidebar** drop-down menu, ensure that **On Left** is selected

5. Enable Volume controls.

    ❏ from the **Controls** area, select **Volume**

    The Volume option adds a volume slider to the Preview area that learners can use to control volume levels. Adding volume controls is a best practice whenever your eLearning includes any kind of audio.

6. Add a logo.

    ❏ from the **Controls** area, select **Logo**

    ❏ click the link **Click to add a logo**

    ❏ from the **Storyline360Data_SecondEdition** folder, open **images_videos**

    ❏ open **CheasapeakeStablesLogo**

7. Reset the Menu.

    ❏ from the top of the dialog box, click **Menu**

NOTES

The order of the slides in the Menu should follow the logical order of the scenes and slides in your project. Prior to publishing or customizing the menu, it's a good idea to **Reset** it.

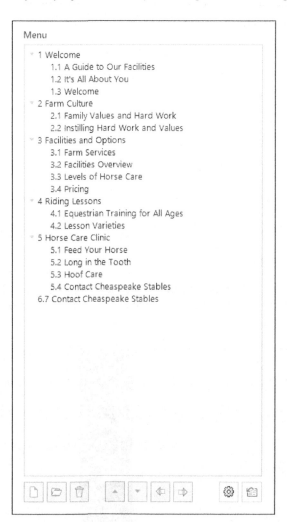

☐ from the bottom right of the menu, click **Reset from Story**

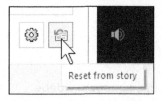

The Reset Menu alert opens.

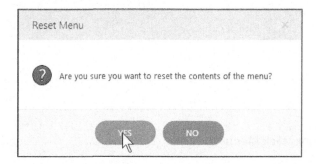

❏ click the **Yes** button

The updated menu includes a few scenes from Story View.

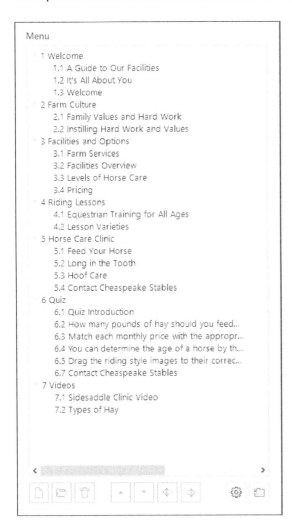

8. Remove an item from the menu.

   ❏ from the Menu, select the **Quiz** scene

   ❏ from the bottom of the menu, click **Delete Heading**

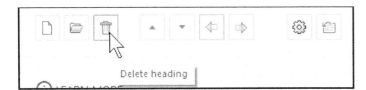

NOTES

You will be prompted to confirm the action.

☐ click the **Remove** button

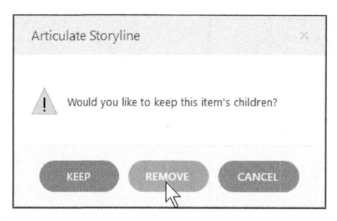

9. Remove another item from the menu.

☐ from the Menu, select the **Videos** scene

☐ from the bottom of the menu, click **Delete Heading**

☐ click the **Remove** button

Your edited menu should look like the picture below.

Menu

▾ 1 Welcome
      1.1 A Guide to Our Facilities
      1.2 It's All About You
      1.3 Welcome
▾ 2 Farm Culture
      2.1 Family Values and Hard Work
      2.2 Instilling Hard Work and Values
▾ 3 Facilities and Options
      3.1 Farm Services
      3.2 Facilities Overview
      3.3 Levels of Horse Care
      3.4 Pricing
▾ 4 Riding Lessons
      4.1 Equestrian Training for All Ages
      4.2 Lesson Varieties
▾ 5 Horse Care Clinic
      5.1 Feed Your Horse
      5.2 Long in the Tooth
      5.3 Hoof Care
      5.4 Contact Cheaspeake Stables

10. Explore the Menu Options.

❏ from the bottom right of the menu, click **Additional Options**

The Menu Options dialog box opens. You are currently looking at the application defaults, and you're going to leave them as is. However, it is worth noting that you can change the Menu from Free to Restricted or Locked. **Free**: Learners can navigate to any part of the course at any time and in any order. **Restricted**: Learners can view the current slide and any slide they have previously viewed, but they can't jump ahead or skip over slides. **Locked**: Learners can view slides only in the order you've designed.

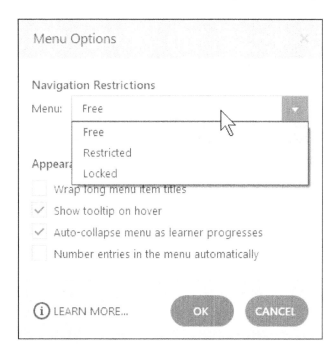

❏ click the **Cancel** button

11. Explore the Classic Player Style.

❏ from the top of the dialog box, **Player Style** area, click the drop-down menu and choose **Classic**

The vast majority of Storyline projects created with Storyline 360 use the Modern Player as opposed to the Classic Player. One big difference between the players is the navigation icons in the lower right of the slide. With the Modern Player, the icons are

simple arrows pointing left and right. With the Classic Player, the icons include text. It is possible to add text to the icons in the Modern Player, which you'll do next.

12. Modify the Modern Player.

☐ from the top of the dialog box, **Appearance** area, click the **Player Style** drop-down menu and choose **Modern**

☐ from the top of the dialog box, click **Colors & Effects**

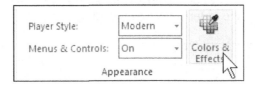

☐ from the **Button Styles** area, **Navigation** drop-down menu, choose **Icon and text**

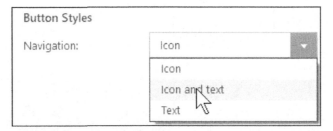

13. Save the changes to the Player Properties.

☐ from the top of the dialog box, click **Current Player** and choose **Save as**

The **Player name** dialog box opens.

❏ change the name to **Chesapeake Stables**

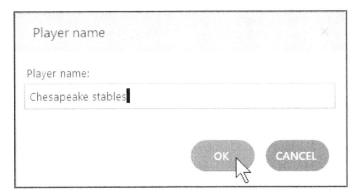

❏ click the **OK** button

❏ click the **OK** button to close the Player screen

14. Save your work.

15. Preview the Entire Project.

   The changes you made to the Player are evident as you move through the lesson.

16. Close the Preview.

Guided Activity 52: Customize Slide Player Features

1. Ensure that the **PublishMe** project is open.

2. Hide the menu for selected slides.

   ☐ switch to **Story View**

   ☐ select slides **1.1, 1.2,** and **1.3**

   ☐ from the lower right of the Storyline window, **Slide Properties** window, click the **Player features** drop-down menu and choose **Custom for the selected slides**

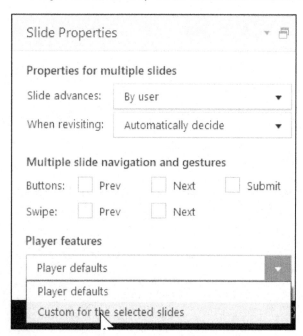

   ☐ **remove** the checkmark from **Menu** (all of the other options should also be deselected)

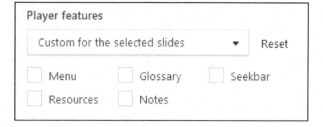

3. Preview the Entire Project.

   Notice that the menu is missing at first. Once you get past Scene 1, the menu magically appears.

4. Close the Preview.

Guided Activity 53: Enable the Seekbar for a Single Slide

1. Ensure that the **PublishMe** project is open.

2. Ensure that you're in Story View.

3. Enable the Seekbar for a single slide.

   ☐ select slide **7.1 Sidesaddle Clinic Video**

   ☐ from the lower right of the Storyline window, **Slide Properties** window, click the **Player features** drop-down menu

   ☐ choose **Custom for the selected slides**

   ☐ deselect any selected options and then select **Seekbar**

   The Seekbar allows learners to see how far they have advanced in any slide. It also allows the learner to fast forward or rewind a slide.

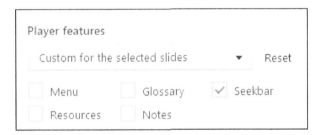

4. Preview slide 7.1.

   The Seekbar appears at the bottom of the slide.

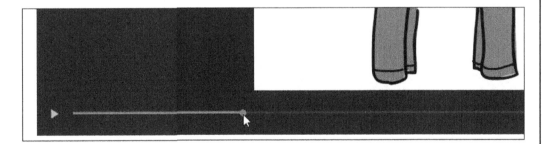

5. Close the Preview.

Guided Activity 54: Use the Media Library to Replace an Image

1. Ensure that the **PublishMe** project is open.

2. Use the Media Library to replace an image.

   ☐ open slide **2.2 Instilling Hard Word & Values**

   You have been asked to replace the **Teaches Responsibility** icon on the slide with an updated icon. Shown below (at the left) is the current Teaches Responsibility icon. The second image shows the updated icon.

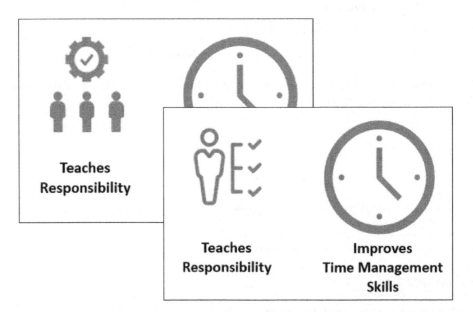

   You could manually delete the image and import a replacement. However, you would also need to resize the new image and position it correctly. As an alternative, you can use the **Media Library** to replace the image with a new one, along with its slide position. In addition, you can replace all instances of the image throughout the project. This is especially useful if you've used the image with Triggers (the Triggers update automatically).

   ☐ select the **View** tab on the Ribbon and click **Media Library**

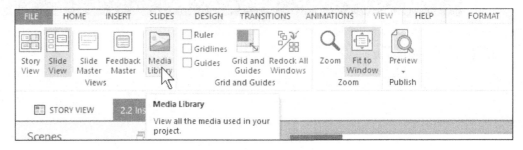

   The Media Library opens.

   ☐ from the top of the Media Library, click **Images**

❏ from the list of images, scroll down and select **responsibility.png**

❏ from the lower right of the Media Library, click **Replace** and choose **Picture from File**

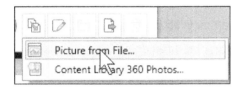

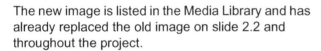

❏ from the **Storyline360Data_SecondEdition > images_videos** folder, open **responsibility-new**

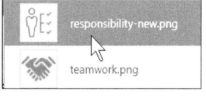

The new image is listed in the Media Library and has already replaced the old image on slide 2.2 and throughout the project.

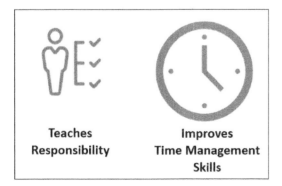

3. Close the Media Library window.

4. Save your work.

Publishing

Once you've added the scenes, slides, images, audio, video, slide objects, and triggers to your project, it's time to make the project available to your learners. This exciting phase of eLearning development is known as Publishing, a process that takes your Storyline project and outputs it into a format that can be viewed by your learners.

The most common way to publish a Storyline project is in HTML5 format. Your learners do **not** need Storyline to view HTML5-published content. Assuming the learner has access to your published content, all that learners need to view the HTML5 is a computer, tablet, or smartphone and a free web browser.

You can publish your Storyline project as a SCORM or AICC content package for use in a LMS, upload your content to Articulate Online (Articulate's LMS), publish as a video, and create handouts of your lesson in Microsoft Word.

Guided Activity 55: Publish Course Content

1. Ensure that the **PublishMe** project is still open.

2. Display the Publish dialog box.

   ☐ choose **File > Publish**

3. Add Project Info.

   ☐ from the left side of the dialog box, ensure that **Web** is selected

   ☐ from the **Title** area, click the **Browse** button (the three dots)

   The Project Info dialog box opens.

   ☐ in the **Author** field, add yourself as the Author

   ☐ in the **Email** field, add your email

   ☐ in the **Website** field, add your corporate or personal website URL

Author:	Kevin Siegel
Email:	manager@chesapeakestables.com
Website:	www.chesapeakestables.com

   ☐ click the **OK** button to return to the Publish dialog box

4. Specify a Publish destination.

   ☐ to the right of **Folder**, click the **Browse** button (the three dots)

   ☐ open the **Storyline360Data_SecondEdition** folder

   ☐ click the **Select Folder** button

Folder:	Desktop\Storyline360Data_2ndEdition

5. Ensure that you are publishing the entire project.

☐ from the **Properties** area, **Publish**, click the link

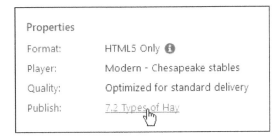

The Publish dialog box opens.

☐ select **Entire project**

☐ click the **OK** button

6. Publish the project.

☐ click the **Publish** button

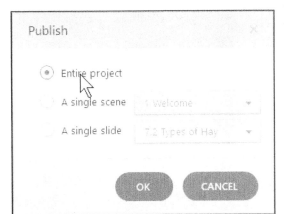

Once the project has been published, the **Publish Successful** dialog box opens. From here you can view the published lesson, FTP the published assets to a web server, zip the assets, email them, or view published lesson.

Note: FTP stands for file transfer protocol, a common standard for moving files across a network or from one computer to another.

☐ click the **View Project** button

The lesson opens in your default web browser. Congratulations, you are now a published eLearning author!

Notice that the project's Title appears in the upper left of the window. You'll remove the title soon.

7. Close the browser and return to Storyline.

   The Publish Successful dialog box should still be open.

8. Observe the Published files.

   ☐ on the **Publish Successful** dialog box, click **Open**

   The Storyline output folder opens. The story.html file is the **start** (home) page. This is the file that your learner will need access to when starting the lesson.

   All of the files in this folder need to be uploaded to your web server together. You should never rename any of the files or change the folder structure (doing so will likely result in the lesson not playing correctly, if at all).

   - html5
   - mobile
   - story_content
   - analytics-frame.html
   - meta.xml
   - story.html

9. Close the window and return to Storyline.

10. Close the Publish Successful dialog box.

Publish Confidence Check

1. Still working in the PublishMe project, open slide **1.1**.

2. Preview the slide.

   Notice that the slide has a navigation button (the Start button) *and* a Next arrow in the lower right of the slide.

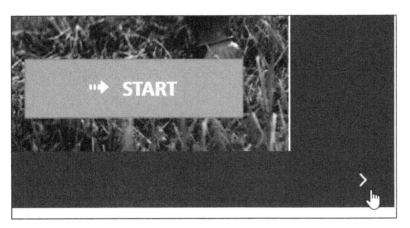

   There will be instances where you want a button for navigation, a Next arrow, or both. In this instance, you want only the slide's Start button, so you'll hide the Next arrow.

3. Close the Preview.

4. Using the **Slide Layers** window, edit the slide's **Properties**

5. Deselect all of the **Slide navigation and gesture** options.

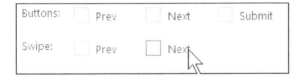

6. Preview slide **1.1** again.

   Notice that the only navigation is the on-board navigation.

7. Close the Preview.

8. Display the **Player Properties**.

9. From the **Features** area, disable the **Title**.

10. Republish the project for the web.

    Notice that the Title has been removed from the upper left of the lesson.

NOTES

11. Close the browser and return to Storyline.

12. Open the **Publish** dialog box.

13. From the list of options at the left, click **Word**.

14. Change the **Screenshot size** to **Large**.

15. **Publish** the output to the **Storyline360Data_SecondEdition** folder.

Properties
✓ Show layers
✓ Show slide notes

Screenshot size: | Large ▼ |

16. View the Document.

You can use this version of your lesson as handouts to support your eLearning course or for additional storyboarding.

1. Welcome

1.1 A Guide to Our Facilities

Notes:

Welcome to Chesapeake Stables. We offer exceptional care for the horse and rider of every discipline.

17. Close the Word document.

18. Save and close the Storyline project.

Congratulations, you're done! We hope you have enjoyed learning some of the more essential skills needed to create killer eLearning content with Articulate Storyline. If you'd like to learn more, check out our Articulate Storyline 360: Beyond the Essentials book. Also, we offer instructor-led Storyline training, live online Storyline mentoring and support, and full eLearning development services on the IconLogic website.

Index

NOTES

Notes

ISBN 978-1-944607-61-6   US$39.00

Made in the USA
Middletown, DE
29 December 2020